The Kent & Sussex Ramblers Guide to
The Wealdway

ISBN: 978-1-906494-32-2

Published by Kent & Sussex Ramblers

www.kentramblers.org.uk

www.sussexramblers.org.uk

© Copyright Ramblers et al 2023

www.ramblers.org.uk

All rights reserved

Contains Ordnance Survey data © Crown copyright 2023

Contains British Geological Survey materials © UKRI 2023

The Ramblers' Association is a registered charity in England & Wales (no: 1093577), a registered charity in Scotland (no: SC039799), and a company limited by guarantee registered in England and Wales (company registration no: 4458492).

Registered office: 13 Dirty Lane, London SE1 9PA

Front cover: Ashdown Forest

This page: Nearing Eastbourne

Contents

Introduction	4
The Landscape of Kent and Sussex	6
Section 1: Gravesend to Sole Street (5.9 miles)	13
Section 2: Sole Street to Platt (9.3 miles)	18
Section 3: Platt to Tonbridge (12.9 miles)	27
Tonbridge Town Trail	32
Section 4: Tonbridge to Speldhurst (6.5 miles)	37
Section 5: Speldhurst to Withyham (6.5 miles)	44
Section 6: Withyham to Five Ash Down (9.1 miles)	51
Section 7: Five Ash Down to East Hoathly (9.0 miles)	59
Section 8: East Hoathly to Upper Horsebridge (6.1 miles)	64
Section 9: Upper Horsebridge to Wilmington (7.1 miles)	69
Section 10: Wilmington to Eastbourne (10.3 miles)	75
Acknowledgements	80
About the Ramblers	80
Waymarking and Signposting	81

Introduction

Welcome to the Wealdway. This 82-mile walk from Gravesend to Eastbourne was opened at a ceremony at Camp Hill on Ashdown Forest in September 1981. It had been nearly a decade in the planning and execution since the Meopham Footpath Group devised a tentative route for the first section from Gravesend to Tonbridge. The project was largely driven by Kent and Sussex Ramblers, and in particular Geoff King, with the support of Kent and East Sussex County Councils.

In contrast with many long distance paths which follow consistent landscape features such as the North and South Downs, the Greensand Ridge and the Medway and Eden river valleys, the Wealdway crosses in turn all of these features as it wends its way from the Thames to the Channel. The walker is therefore able to see how landscape changes with underlying geology, how different the ecology of the sandstones of the High Weald is from that of the chalk Downs and how different have been the economic and social histories of the various regions. It is also interesting to note not just the similarities but also the differences in the characters of the North and South Downs, despite their shared geology.

Apart from Tonbridge, the Wealdway does not pass through any towns between Gravesend and Eastbourne. It feels very remote in places as it passes through quiet villages and open country. This remoteness has just one downside – the Wealdway is less well served by public transport than many long-distance walks. Despite this, we have sought to break the route into sections of no more than ten miles that are served by public transport at both ends. We have not quite succeeded – there are a section of 12.9 miles and a section of 10.3 miles. It is possible to split both of these sections into shorter ones accessible by public transport and there is advice on doing so in the text but in neither case is the split ideal and we expect that most walkers will want to make a special effort to complete them at one go.

The Wealdway is reasonably well waymarked. Where there were particular problems, Ramblers' volunteers have been out and fixed them. In particular the original waymarking across Ashdown Forest was in poor condition so Sussex Ramblers installed a series of new posts in the summer of 2021 in preparation for the celebration of the 40th anniversary of the walk. The waymarks are a little sparse as you approach Eastbourne but by that stage the Wealdway is following the South Downs Way so you can follow the signs and waymarks for that.

Maps

Much effort has gone into the maps included in the book to ensure that they are clear and accurate and they should be adequate for following the route. However, the Ordnance Survey 1:25,000 Explorer maps cover a much larger area and enable you to see a wider picture and context. The ones that cover the Wealdway are 163, 148, 136, 147, 135 and OL25. However, at the time of writing some of these maps have not been updated for many years whereas those in this book are believed to be up to date as at April 2023.

Planning and Equipment

The route is described as a series of one day walks with public transport options at each end. The public transport arrangements aren't always ideal and as provision is liable to change you are advised to check timetables carefully on www.traveline.info. Some walkers will wish to use two cars if these are available and there is always the option of the occasional taxi. Finally you could walk from the start of a section to the middle and then back and likewise from the end – the route will seem very different walked in the opposite direction.

We have not provided details of accommodation for those wishing to do the whole route at one go as such information becomes out of date quickly. However, if readers would like to recommend suitable places to stay, we will consider putting the details on the Kent Ramblers' web site.

The Weald is famed for its mud. This does usually dry out in summer but a prolonged downpour can soon revive it. The wearing of boots is therefore strongly advised. You should also take your waterproofs, sun hat, sun cream, sunglasses, mobile phone and camera.

There are refreshment possibilities at the start and finish of most sections but not a lot in between so you should take ample provisions with you.

Safety

Walking, especially in lowland areas, is a pretty safe activity. The biggest danger is when crossing or briefly walking along a busy road with no pavement or verge, which is sometimes unavoidable. Keep to the right-hand side and be prepared to walk in single file. At a sharp right-hand bend it may be safer to cross to the left-hand side of the road and cross back after the bend. For more safety advice see www.ramblers.org.uk/go-walking-hub/safety.

Wherever you walk, you should consider taking precautions against ticks that may transmit Lyme disease.

Other Walking Opportunities

There are many splendid walks in Kent and Sussex with more details on Kent and Sussex Ramblers' web sites. Other guides to named walks published by Kent Ramblers are shown below and more are planned. All profits from these guides are used to promote and improve these walks and carry out other work for the benefit of walkers in Kent and Sussex.

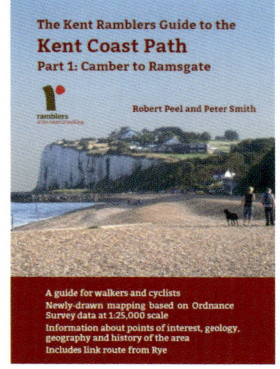
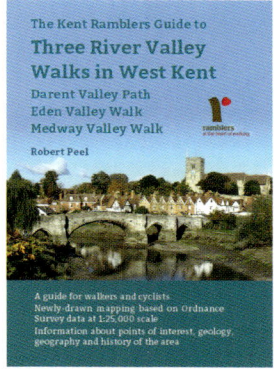
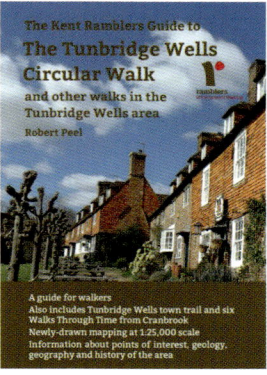

The Landscape of Kent and Sussex

Geology

The landscape crossed by the Wealdway is very much defined in terms of underlying geology. Most of the solid rocks exposed in Kent and large parts of Sussex were laid down under water during a geological period known as the Cretaceous which began around 144 million years ago.

Beneath the rocks of the Cretaceous are older rocks of the Jurassic and earlier geological periods including coal measures that were once exploited in the collieries of east Kent.

As the Cretaceous began, the platform of Jurassic and older rocks in the area had subsided and been covered by the waters of a large estuary whose boundaries changed over the millennia so that sediments washed down by the river sometimes settled in freshwater and sometimes in saltwater.

Figure 1

Over time huge beds of sandstones, mudstones and occasionally limestones built up until, around 97 million years ago, much of the area was inundated by the sea and thick layers of chalk built up from the bodies of marine creatures that settled to the seabed.

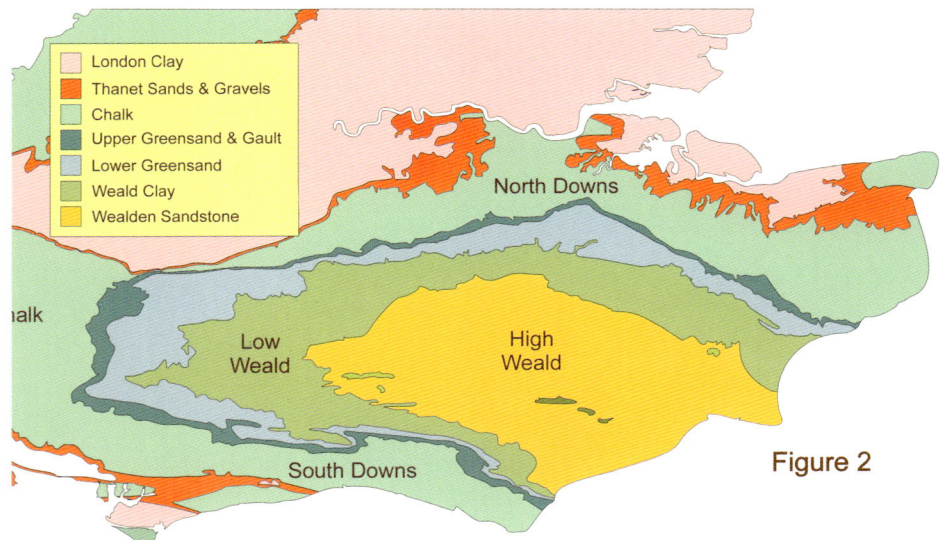

Figure 2

Figure 1 (top) shows the sequence of the beds that had built up by the end of the Cretaceous around 66 million years ago. The colour scheme is the same as that of figure 2.

At this time the uplift of the Weald began, being initially very limited but sufficient to raise the area above sea level and so halt the deposition of the chalk.

Gradually the pressure from the tectonic processes creating the Alps increased until by 10 to 20 million years ago a roughly west to east anticline (ridge) was forming. At the same time there was pressure from the west due to the opening of the North Atlantic so that the net result was an elongated dome that covered not just south east England but also what is now the English Channel and parts of north west Europe – Figure 1 (middle).

As this dome was eroded away the oldest rocks were exposed in the centre and the youngest rocks at the edge forming a series of concentric oval rings – figures 1 (bottom) and 2. The chalk was the outermost ring, forming the North and South Downs and corresponding outcrops on the other side of the Channel. The inner rings – the Weald Clay and the Wealden Sandstone (or Hastings Beds) – are often referred to respectively as the Low Weald and the High Weald.

Landscape & Geology

The Wealdway crosses all the concentric rings – all but the central one twice – see figure 3 on next page which shows a cross-section through the whole structure along the exact line of the Wealdway, the vertical dimension much exaggerated compared to the horizontal.

The North Downs

Climbing out of Gravesend and across the A2, you are on the chalk of the North Downs and, although there are both ups and downs, the general trend is upwards along the side of one of the dry valleys that characterise the northern side of the North Downs ridge. Because chalk is porous it is not now possible for streams to form and erode valleys but during the last ice age, although glaciers did not reach Kent, the ground was frozen so that water flowed across the surface forming streams and eroding the chalk to create the now dry valleys. After reaching the top, the descent of the south facing escarpment is far steeper than the ascent, crossing the North Downs Way and passing the Coldrum Stones long barrow on the way down.

Although The North and South Downs are part of the same chalk formation, they have strikingly different characters. There are three main reasons for the differences. Firstly substantial parts of the North Downs are covered in deposits known as "clay with flints" whose origin is much debated. These deposits, which are much less prevalent

Scarp slope of North Downs

on the South Downs, made cultivation difficult with the result that clearance of woodland was much slower on the North Downs than on the South Downs. Secondly the proximity to London resulted in more settlement and a recreational element, including a trend that we might today call "hobby farming", in the exploitation of the North Downs developing earlier than in the case of the South Downs. Thirdly the escarpment of the North Downs faces south so that at the foot of the escarpment where a spring line forms at the boundary with the Gault clay there is a warm and sheltered microclimate where continental species of plants thrive. The equivalent position in the South Downs, north facing and cooler, is more suited to oceanic species.

Gault

The Upper Greensand is scarcely present but the Gault clay forms a long depression running West-East at the foot of the Downs known as the Vale of Holmesdale. In 1846, eminent agriculturalist George Buckland described the vale as lying "under the sunny side of the chalk hills like the forward border under the lee of a garden wall". The clay may be hard to work but it produces good crops of legumes, cereals and especially hops.

Lower Greensand Quarry

The M26 follows the Vale very closely but after merging with the M20 the motorway bears slightly south of the Gault into the uppermost layer of the Lower Greensand so that the Wealdway crosses the Gault just before reaching the M20, specifically in Ryarsh Wood.

Lower Greensand

Just south of Ryarsh Wood the Wealdway passes, and may be temporally diverted around, a huge hole in the ground from which sand from a layer of Lower Greensand, known as the

Figure 3: Cross-section of Kent and East Sussex along the exact line of the Wealdway. The vertical scale is considerably exaggerated compared with the horizontal scale.

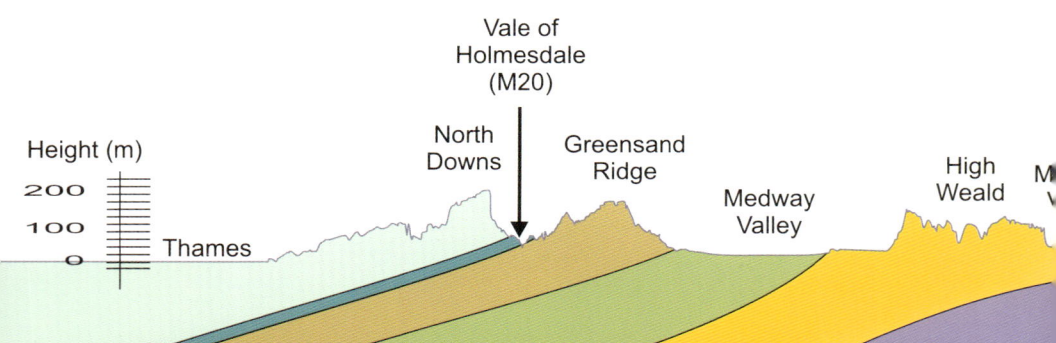

Folkestone Formation, is at the time of writing being quarried. The Wealdway continues across the Lower Greensand through Mereworth Woods until, soon after passing through West Peckham, it reaches the Weald Clay.

Weald Clay

Historically this section of the Weald Clay was very much hop-growing territory and former oast houses abound. Here the Medway runs through the clay and soon the Wealdway is following its banks into Tonbridge.

The High Weald

Wealden Ghyll

By the time you reach Tonbridge you are in the High Weald with sandstone beneath your feet. This remains the case for many miles to come as the Wealdway, after crossing the meandering Medway a couple more times west of Groombridge, begins the long ascent to the top of the Wealden dome at Ashdown Forest. From here, after taking in the panoramic views, there is a steep descent followed by many smaller ups and downs before you leave the High Weald as you arrive at Upper Horsebridge on the outskirts of Hailsham.

The alternating sandstone ridges and clay valleys have historically made the High Weald a difficult landscape for agriculture, especially the growing of crops. Prior to the Roman occupation the Weald was covered by a large forest (a mixture of woodland with clearings of grassland and heath), the Andredsweald, which was lightly exploited for timber and iron ore and some grazing. The Romans developed a vibrant iron industry which consumed large quantities of timber but after their departure the industry waned and the forest reclaimed much of the cleared land.

Sandy heath of Ashdown Forest

Elsewhere in Britain the post-glacial forests were cleared much more quickly than that covering the Weald – in 1086 the High Weald was the most densely wooded area in England. On the North and South Downs and adjacent coastal plains, arable farming became widespread with estates and villages whose occupants in Saxon times herded their animals, especially pigs, into the Weald in autumn to fatten on the profusion of acorns. This practice, known as pannage, continued over centuries, repeatedly using the same routes which became worn down by feet and trotters to create sunken tracks or "routeways" that survive to this day as paths and lanes.

Low Weald Pasture

Each farm would set up a settlement, or "den", in the High Weald, initially a temporary affair for the pannage season. Gradually these settlements became permanent and their occupants began to cut back the woodland sufficiently to accommodate a home and to create small fields for pasture and for a few subsistence crops. The names of many places in the Weald reflect these origins – Tenterden, Horsmonden and Rolvenden for example.

By the 14th century pannage was a thing of the past and the pattern of small farmsteads with a mixture of pasture, crops for personal consumption and thin strips of woodland separating small fields was well established. This pattern is still apparent today, making the High Weald the best preserved medieval landscape in northern Europe.

Agriculture in the High Weald was never very lucrative and the wealth that funded the fine houses nestling in the intimate landscape came from other sources. In particular there was a thriving woollen cloth industry from the 14th to the 17th centuries while in the 16th and 17th centuries the Wealden iron industry operated on a massive scale providing much of Britain's iron and in particular its guns and cannon. Accordingly a substantial proportion of the fine timber-framed and stone houses in the Weald were built by master weavers and iron masters. The iron industry also left a legacy of ponds built to store water to drive forge hammers and furnace bellows and these too are an important part of landscape character.

The industry has gone but the woods, the patchwork of small fields dominated by pasture, the fine medieval and Tudor houses, the ponds and the sunken routeways remain. These are what define the Weald and make it such an attractive destination for the discerning walker. The mud remains too and while not so welcome it is a small price to pay for its role in impeding development that might otherwise have ruined this special landscape.

Weald Clay, Greensand and Gault

The route crosses Weald Clay until just south of Arlington where it crosses a band of Lower Greensand less than half a mile wide, soon traversing a narrow strip of Gault.

The South Downs

As Britain emerged from the last ice age, the soon-wooded South Downs offered perhaps its most hospitable landscape to early man arriving from the continent. Once trees were felled, soon achieved with tools made from the plentiful supply of locally available flints, the light soils were easily cultivated. The soils were thin, however, and to make them more fertile a system developed that mixed arable and sheep grazing. The sheep were brought from their daytime pasture on the higher ground into the cultivated fields below at night to deposit their dung and trample it into the soil. In Roman times there would have been farming settlements all along the chalk ridge but in Saxon times these were abandoned and habitation became concentrated in larger villages at the foot of the Downs. The mixture of sheep grazing and cultivation, particularly cereals, remained at the heart of Downland agriculture for some 5000 years until the early 20th century.

By the 1920s the South Downs had become a national icon, widely seen as encapsulating all that is best in an English rural landscape. But the next fifty years were not kind to the Downs, the needs of wartime leading to extensive ploughing up and enclosure of formerly open grassland for the growing of crops. Post-war agricultural policy did little to slow, let alone reverse, this damaging trend so that by 1957 the recreational value of the landscape was no longer thought great enough for designation as a National Park. It took more than fifty years to reverse that view but now we have a National Park Authority to help tackle the many challenges faced by this historic landscape.

Northern scarp of South Downs near Wilmington

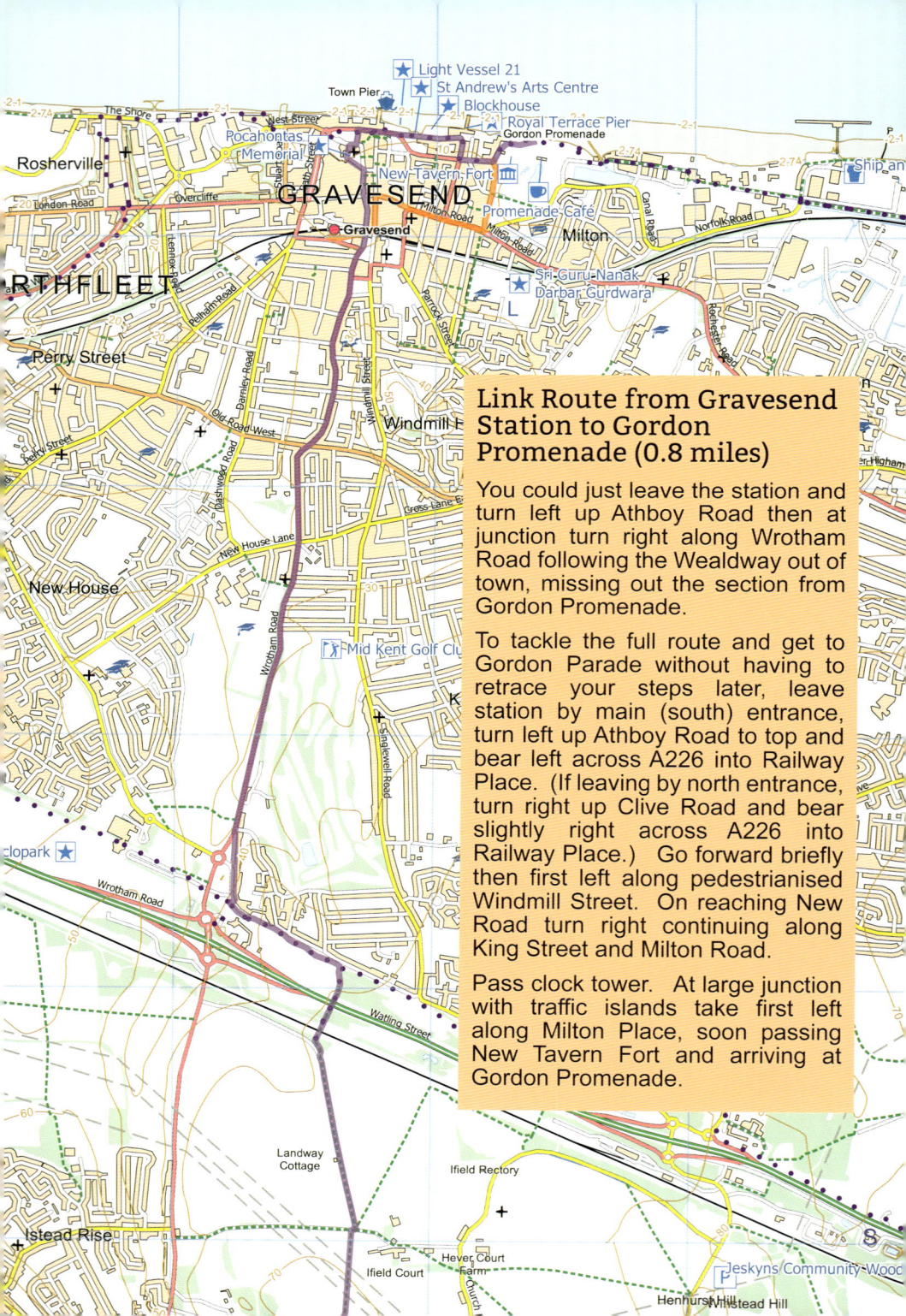

Link Route from Gravesend Station to Gordon Promenade (0.8 miles)

You could just leave the station and turn left up Athboy Road then at junction turn right along Wrotham Road following the Wealdway out of town, missing out the section from Gordon Promenade.

To tackle the full route and get to Gordon Parade without having to retrace your steps later, leave station by main (south) entrance, turn left up Athboy Road to top and bear left across A226 into Railway Place. (If leaving by north entrance, turn right up Clive Road and bear slightly right across A226 into Railway Place.) Go forward briefly then first left along pedestrianised Windmill Street. On reaching New Road turn right continuing along King Street and Milton Road.

Pass clock tower. At large junction with traffic islands take first left along Milton Place, soon passing New Tavern Fort and arriving at Gordon Promenade.

Section 1: Gravesend to Sole Street (5.9 miles)

From Gordon Promenade with Thames on your right follow England Coast Path signage to left between mound protecting New Tavern Fort from river and building belonging to Gravesend Rowing Club. Follow round to left and at road junction turn right along The Terrace. At crossroads turn right down Royal Pier Road, passing Royal Terrace Pier as you bear left at the bottom. Continue along Royal Pier Road, noting the brick remains of Gravesend Blockhouse opposite Clarendon Hotel as you pass. Pass St Andrews Arts Centre, go up steps (noting red Light Vessel 21 to your right), now leaving the Coast Path, to join Crooked Lane. Go forward past Gravesend Town Pier on right and continue to next road junction. Turn left towards St George's church, turn right in front of church then left into churchyard where you will find statue of Pocahontas. Pass to right of statue then bear left alongside St George's Shopping Centre (where there are toilets). On reaching Princes Street, turn right to cross New Road, a main shopping street.

Go straight across up Stone Street soon passing Clive Road leading to railway station on right. Press on along Stone Street, which soon becomes Wrotham Road. Follow this road for nearly two miles until close to A2, visible ahead. Immediately after passing Chalky Bank on the left, as Wrotham Road starts to bear right towards roundabout, bear slightly left along access road and past concrete bollards. Cross road where it turns left towards filling station, through cyclebarrier into Cyclopark, turn left joining shared cycle path 177 and continue past filling station. Through barrier keep left at fork and continue along shared cycle path, possibly the line of the Roman Road known as Watling Street.

After 450 metres take path on right through gap in bank signed "Ifield Court", cross bridge over A2 ("hare bridge" on account of the steel figures decorating it) and HS1 railway bridge and on reaching track at T-junction bear left along it. Follow track away from A2 for 700 metres to T-junction. Turn right and immediately left.

Follow left hand edge of field, at corner turn right and at next corner go through gap in hedge and turn left along path descending along left hand edge of very large field. After lowest point follow path slightly into edge of wood where it starts climbing, with wood on left then between hedges – follow all the way to lane at Nash Street.

Turn left and when lane ends continue forward along bridleway. At junction of paths turn left just before gate, still following bridleway, downhill with wood on left and hedge on right and then up again. Keep forward at junctions on enclosed path with woodland on left and fields on right to Copt Hall Road.

Take path opposite along left hand edge of field. At corner bear left through woodland and diagonally across next field to White Post Lane.

Turn right and after 50 metres take path on left. At T-junction turn left, soon reaching Manor Road. Turn right and follow to T-junction at top by parish hall and with village shop opposite. Turn right along Sole Street, over railway bridge and right to railway station.

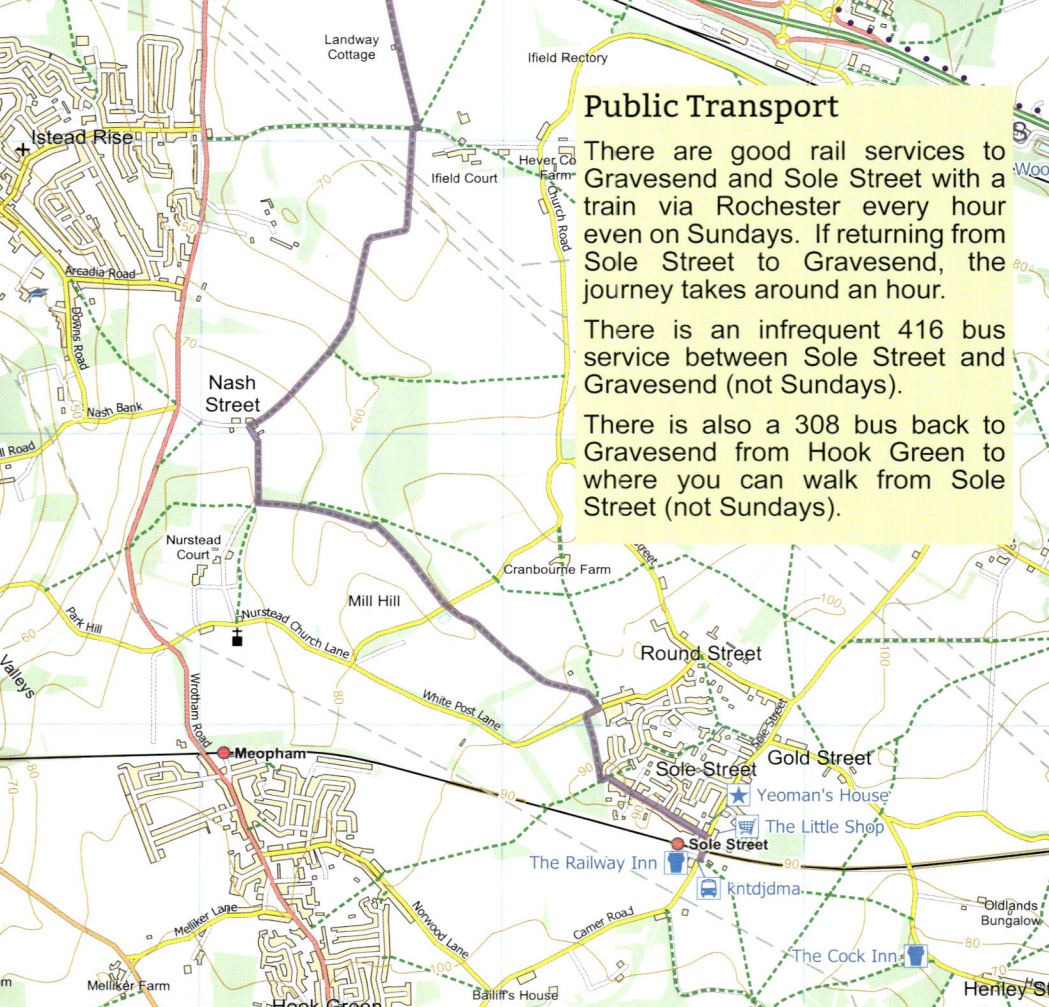

Points of Interest

New Tavern Fort

Although there had been fortifications here since the 1780s, the surviving structures were largely built in the 1860s under the direction of Colonel Gordon, later General Gordon of Khartoum fame. The earthworks and gun emplacements are now a public park while the extensive tunnels are open on Sunday afternoons in the summer months.

Royal Terrace Pier

Built in 1844, later roofed over and now part of the headquarters of the London Port Authority. It acquired the description "Royal" after Princess Alexandra landed here in 1865 on her way to marry the Prince of Wales.

St Andrew's Arts Centre

Called St Andrew's Waterside Chapel when opened in 1871 to serve the local seafaring community, the building was largely financed by the daughter of Rear Admiral Francis Beaufort who invented the Beaufort Scale for defining wind speeds. Beaufort played a leading role in the search for his friend Sir John Franklin who died in an ill-fated expedition to find the Northwest Passage. The church, now an arts centre, contains a memorial to the sailors of Franklin's two ships, HMS Erebus and HMS Terror.

Light Vessel 21

The LV21 Lightship was built in 1963, survived a severe collision with a ship under tow in the Strait of Dover in 1981 and was decommissioned in 2008. It has now been converted into a venue for meetings, performances and art exhibitions.

Town Pier

Originally built in 1834, this is the world's oldest surviving cast iron pier. Restored from dereliction by Gravesham Council in 2002, the pier and attached pontoon offer ferry services to Tilbury at roughly 30 minute intervals (but no service on Sundays or bank holidays). If you have a National Concessionary Bus Pass you can travel free after 9:30am.

Pocahontas Memorial

One of Gravesend's main claims to fame is as the burial place of Pocahontas, daughter of an American Indian chieftain. She saved the life of the president of Virginia, married an Englishman, came to England, was received in court and died on board a ship off Gravesend at the start of her voyage home. She was also the subject of a 1995 Disney movie which, while very popular, took some liberties with historical accuracy.

Sri Guru Nanak Darbar Gurdwara

Said to be Europe's largest and finest Sikh place of worship.

Cyclopark

The Cyclopark was built in 2011 after the A2 had been moved 200 metres to the south to run alongside the Channel Tunnel Rail link and away from local housing. The Cyclopark car park is on the line of the old road and the Cyclopark itself is sandwiched between the old and new road lines. Facilities are oriented towards family activities including various cycling, skating and fitness classes. The enterprise is run by a charity.

Ifield Court

You don't get more than a glimpse of this Grade II listed building as you pass. It is largely 18th century built in brown brick but it does incorporate remains of a 15th century manor house.

The Leather Bottle

Nurstead Court

The 13th century aisled timbered hall built by Bishop Stephen de Gravesend survived intact until 1825 when half was demolished to make way for a stuccoed brick villa, now operated as a wedding venue.

Church of St Mildred, Nurstead

The small 14th century church has a simple and elegant interior that makes it popular for weddings. St Mildred lived from around 660 to 730 and was Abbess at Minster-in-Thanet in East Kent.

Yeoman's House, Sole Street

Just a few metres' detour to your left when you arrive opposite the village shop in Sole Street is a 15th century timber-framed house restored by architect Sir Herbert Baker (who lived at Owletts see below) and given to the National Trust in 1931. It is occupied by a tenant with no public access.

Cobham

Although not on the Wealdway, this picturesque village is only a five minute drive from Sole Street and worth a visit if time allows. One of its main claims to fame is that its ancient inn, the Leather Bottle, was frequented by Charles Dickens and is featured in Pickwick Papers as "a clean commodious village ale-house". The inn plays heavily on its Dickensian connections to attract and please the tourist trade.

The **church of St Mary Magdelene** is famed for what is said to be the finest collection of Medieval brasses in the world dating from 1320 to 1529. Fourteen of these relate to members of the Cobham family who died out in the reign of James I but had already made a huge contribution to the locality. The brasses, at one time

Cobham College

Cobham Tomb

stored away in chests, were laid in their present position on the floor in the 19th century.

Also of note in the church is the tomb of the 9th Lord Cobham and his wife bearing beautifully carved alabaster effigies.

Behind the church is Cobham College, founded in 1362 as a chantry employing five priests. After the dissolution of the monasteries it lay vacant for a while until in 1597 the 10th Lord Cobham funded their conversion into almshouses. The building is still run by a charity offering low cost retirement accommodation for former residents of nearby parishes.

Not far away is **Cobham Hall**, a magnificent Elizabethan brick mansion built in 1584 to 1602. Charles I and his bride Henrietta Maria spent their honeymoon night here. The house is now a girls' boarding school and is only open to the public on a few days a year, advertised on the school's web site.

In the former grounds of the hall is the **Darnley mausoleum** which fell into disrepair but was rescued with £4.9 million of lottery funding awarded in 2004. It is now owned by the National Trust and is typically open two Sundays a month from June to September. It can be viewed externally from public footpaths including the Darnley Trail, a 6.2 mile circular route for walkers, cyclists and horse riders from Shorne Woods Country Park that also passes through Jeskyns open space.

Owletts

Also in Cobham is **Owletts**, a red-brick country house dating from the 1830s although much altered especially during the occupation of renowned architect Sir Herbert Baker. The gardens were partly designed by Gertrude Jekyll and the property is now owned by the National Trust and let to tenants. The house is particularly noted for its first floor ornate plaster ceiling from 1684 depicting scrolls, leaves, flowers and fruit. It is currently open to the public on a few days a year but at the time of writing the current tenants are about to leave and future opening arrangements are uncertain.

The Thames from Gordon Promenade

Section 2: Sole Street to Platt (9.3 miles)

From railway station head up access road to Camer Road, cross and turn right. When road starts to bear right, take track on left (not track into Camer Park which is closer to straight ahead), then keeping right with woodland on right and open fields on left. Follow track round left hand bend then gently right past a few houses. After section of woodland (Henley Wood) on right, cross junction of four paths, follow left hand edge of open field (going under powerlines) then go through short section of woodland into vineyard. Head down right hand side of vineyard to gate and steps into field. Turn left along top of field, soon becoming a vineyard, and after 190 metres at bench on left turn right down path through vineyard. Beyond bottom, head uphill keeping to right of line of trees ahead. Go through gate and woodland to emerge through hedge onto Oakenden Lane.

Go straight across up steps, cross field to protruding corner of hedge and turn left with hedge on right. Continue to corner, down steps and emerge at junction of lanes at Luddesdown. Turn right along private drive past church on right and old barn on left. After right hand bend in drive go through gate on left, down very small field and into to large field.

Head to top corner of field past metal gate on left, bear right then go through second metal gate (adjacent to field gate) into vineyard. Bear right along top of vineyard for 530 metres then pass through metal gate into meadow. Bear slighty left to gate and in next field follow gently descending path parallel to vineyard on left. At next gate enter another vineyard now with vines on both sides; continue to gate 40 metres to left of corner and go up steps into Buckland Road.

Turn right to road junction then fork right down Lockyers Hill. Pass Great Buckland Farm on right and continue uphill to first bend. Go through gate on left into wood and follow clear track through wood to emerge into open field. Follow right hand edge of field then bear right along track between fences. At end cross private drive to go through gate, across paddock and over stile onto Leywood Road.

Turn left along lane for 350 metres to first bend. Go through gap ahead and along left hand edge of field. Go through first gap on left then sharp right with tree line on right and woodland on left. Soon emerge into open field and follow right hand edge to corner then over stile and along enclosed path to White Horse Road at Poundgate Farm.

Turn right and after 75 metres take signposted path on left into wood. Follow path through wood, going straight across any other paths or tracks. At edge of North Downs escarpment, take descending path ahead although it doesn't initially look very promising, soon (after about 50 metres) bear right, gradually descend to several sets of steps and emerge on the North Downs Way. Turn right for a few metres passing junction where North Downs Way goes off on right, then take path on left down steps, signposted to Coldrum Longbarrow.

Follow clear descending path along right hand edge of very large field until you reach barrow on right. After visiting barrow continue in same direction as before but when path surface becomes concrete and bears

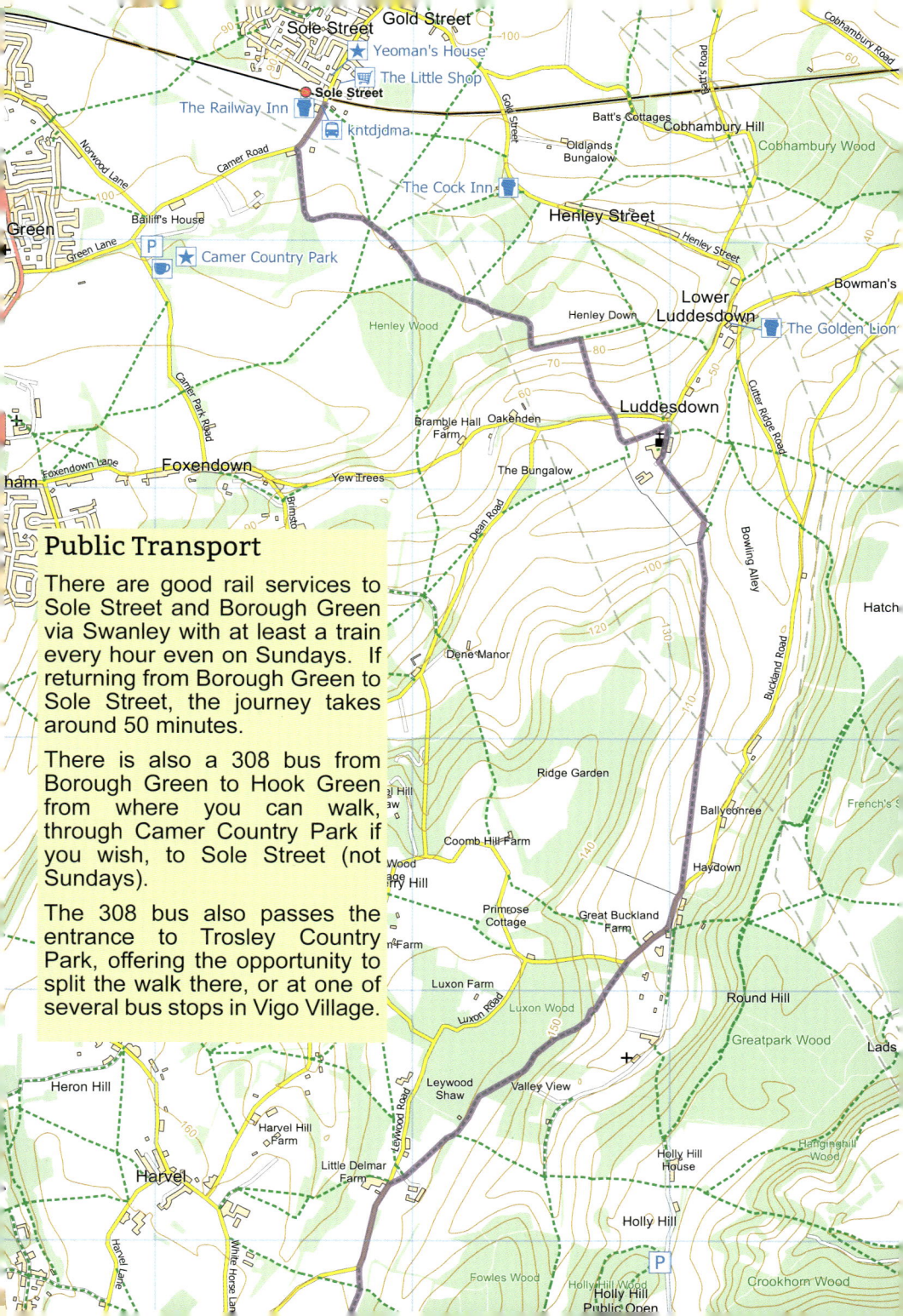

Public Transport

There are good rail services to Sole Street and Borough Green via Swanley with at least a train every hour even on Sundays. If returning from Borough Green to Sole Street, the journey takes around 50 minutes.

There is also a 308 bus from Borough Green to Hook Green from where you can walk, through Camer Country Park if you wish, to Sole Street (not Sundays).

The 308 bus also passes the entrance to Trosley Country Park, offering the opportunity to split the walk there, or at one of several bus stops in Vigo Village.

right, take path on left at corner into scrub. At junction of tracks, bear left towards gate opposite and continue in same direction through Ryarsh Wood. On emerging into field, turn left with edge of wood on left. When wood ends continue along field edge to corner and go through gate.

At time of writing path on ground goes straight forward alongside fence to join Woodgate Road at junction with Addington Lane. However, path has been legally diverted to go left after just a few metres along field edge then right at corner down to Woodgate Road about 130 metres from junction, requiring right turn along road to junction. The diversion is to allow quarry on right to be extended across original (and at time of writing current) line of path; presumably when this happens diversion on map will be put into effect on ground.

Turn right along Addington Lane for 340 metres and as lane bears right take path on left just after quarry entrance. Follow through trees then with care across two quarry tracks down to tunnel under M20.

Turn immediately right up path parallel to motorway, later bearing left through wood and down steps to private drive at Westfields Farm. Bear left along drive briefly then right along path soon leading to St Vincents Lane.

Turn right and follow lane for 545 metres descending to stream and then climbing again to take path up steps on right immediately past Brookfield House. Follow path, with woodland on left and fine views across fields to the North Downs on the right, to Ford Lane.

Go straight across and follow path gradually climbing and bearing gently left at junction to London Road (A20) at Wrotham Heath.

Cross busy road carefully and bear right for a very short distance to take track between Royal Oak Beefeater and Ming Restaurant, soon going under railway, and follow in same direction to Windmill Hill.

Turn left for 250 metres then take path on right well hidden in shrubbery adjacent to second drive on right. Follow path initially between fences into wood. At junction in paths go straight ahead for 20 metres to regain and then keep fence on left to emerge on private drive. Turn left for a few metres along path beside drive to Comp Lane.

Turn right and take first left along Potash Lane. At junction with small triangular green either turn right to follow link route to Borough Green station or go forward to continue along Wealdway.

Points of Interest

Camer Country Park

The park covers 46 acres of parkland and woodland and there is a small café. It is noted for its wildlife, particularly slow worms and common lizards. The park is very popular with dog owners, which some visitors find off-putting. The mature parkland was once the grounds of Camer House, formerly the home of the Smith-Masters family, built in the 17th and 18th centuries and now Grade II listed. The estate was sold to Strood Council in 1967 and later transferred to Kent County Council but the house was retained in private ownership and is now divided into several dwellings. The Camer Estate Book of 1726-44 survives and is a valuable source of information about farming practices on the North Downs at the time.

Bowling Alley

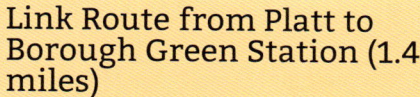

Link Route from Platt to Borough Green Station (1.4 miles)

Bear right at the green along Boneashe Lane and then left along Comp Lane, after 300 metres becoming Long Mill Lane. Continue past church. When Grange Road forks to right, keep to left fork along Long Mill Lane and continue past The Blue Anchor pub on your right to Maidstone Road (A25). Turn left and follow for 950 metres, passing The Black Horse pub on your left, to Station Road on right (one way street with No Entry signs). Station Road, as you might expect, leads to the station. However, it is narrow and without a footway so you may prefer to continue along Maidstone Road to crossroads and turn right up High Street to station, although this is a little longer.

Luddesdown Court and Church

Luddesdown Court

Some claim that Bishop Odo, half-brother of William the Conqueror, once lived here and that it is the oldest continuously occupied house in England. Certainly Odo owned the land but the Grade I listing details with Historic England suggest that the house itself was built in the early 13th century whereas Odo died in 1097.

Bowling Alley

Back in the 1980s the Ministry of Defence bought this splendid, sweeping dry valley to use as a training area for tank drivers. Volunteers from Kent Ramblers and other local amenity groups launched such an effective campaign against the proposal that the MOD gave up and sold the land so that walkers continue to enjoy it today. Views will no doubt differ on the aesthetics of the vines that now cover the valley, but they are certainly preferable to mines and tanks.

Silverhand Vineyard

This vineyard is one of the largest in the UK with 230 hectares of vines planted in 2019. The vineyard is organic, hence the sheep to be seen grazing grass and weeds between the rows of vines, fertilising as they go. The wines produced appear to be sparkling whites.

The Lost Village of Dode

The village was abandoned after most of its inhabitants were wiped out by the Black Death in 1348. Nothing now remains except for the small Norman church and even this is largely reconstructed, much of the original stone having been used in the building of a nearby medieval church. The church is privately owned and operated as a wedding venue. The stone circle in the churchyard is a twenty-first century construction.

Trosley Country Park

As you cross the North Downs Way you are close to the very eastern tip of the park. Unfortunately the café and toilets are at the far western end and a detour to visit them would take over an hour. The park contains a mixture of woodland and chalk downland, the latter being managed with the help of a herd of goats to encourage the many native wildflowers.

Pilgrims Way and North Downs Way

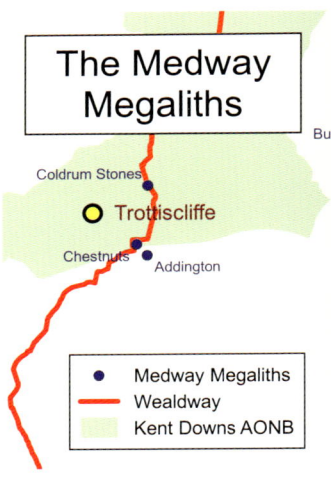

At the point you reach it, the Pilgrims Way coincides with the North Downs Way but by the time you leave it mere seconds later the routes have separated, the former continuing at the same level and the latter heading steeply uphill. The Pilgrims Way connects Winchester and London to Canterbury, the two routes merging at Kemsing. In general the Pilgrims Way follows contours halfway down the southern escarpment of the North Downs, roughly along the spring line, while the North Downs Way tends to follow a higher route where possible. Although the Pilgrims Way is associated with the tales of Chaucer, the route has much older origins as an ancient trackway.

The North Downs Way runs for around 140 miles from Farnham in Surrey to Dover including an optional loop to take in Canterbury. From Canterbury to Dover, the route coincides with that of the Via Francigena, another pilgrim route that continues across the Channel and finishes in Rome.

The Hartley Morris Men welcome the sunrise on Mayday at the Coldrum Stones

Coldrum Stones (Long Barrow)

The Coldrum long barrow is the best-preserved of a group of Neolithic barrows known as the Medway Megaliths, the most studied of which are shown on the map below. Little is known about the culture that built the barrows around a thousand years before Stonehenge was built.

The Medway barrows are classified as chambered megaliths – they are constructed of both stone and earth which distinguishes them from the long barrows of east Kent which consist solely of earthen mounds. As far as is known, the chamber of the barrow extended only about 4.5 metres into the mound from the eastern end while the full length of the mound was 20 metres.

Most of the stones at the east end of the Coldrum barrow, including the capstone of the chamber, have fallen down the embankment towards the track along which the Wealdway passes. It is thought that this was a deliberate act of damage undertaken in the 11th century, possibly part of a wider project to erase what were believed to be heathen monuments and strengthen the hold of Christianity on society.

The Coldrum barrow is the only member of the Medway group where substantial human remains have been found – when excavated in 1910 it was found to contain the remains of at least 17 individuals including adults and children. The bodies had been dismembered and the bones rearranged.

The site is used for various pagan rituals and every May Day local Morris men perform here as the sun rises. Since 1926 it has been in the care of the National Trust.

Tentative Model of Original Long Barrow

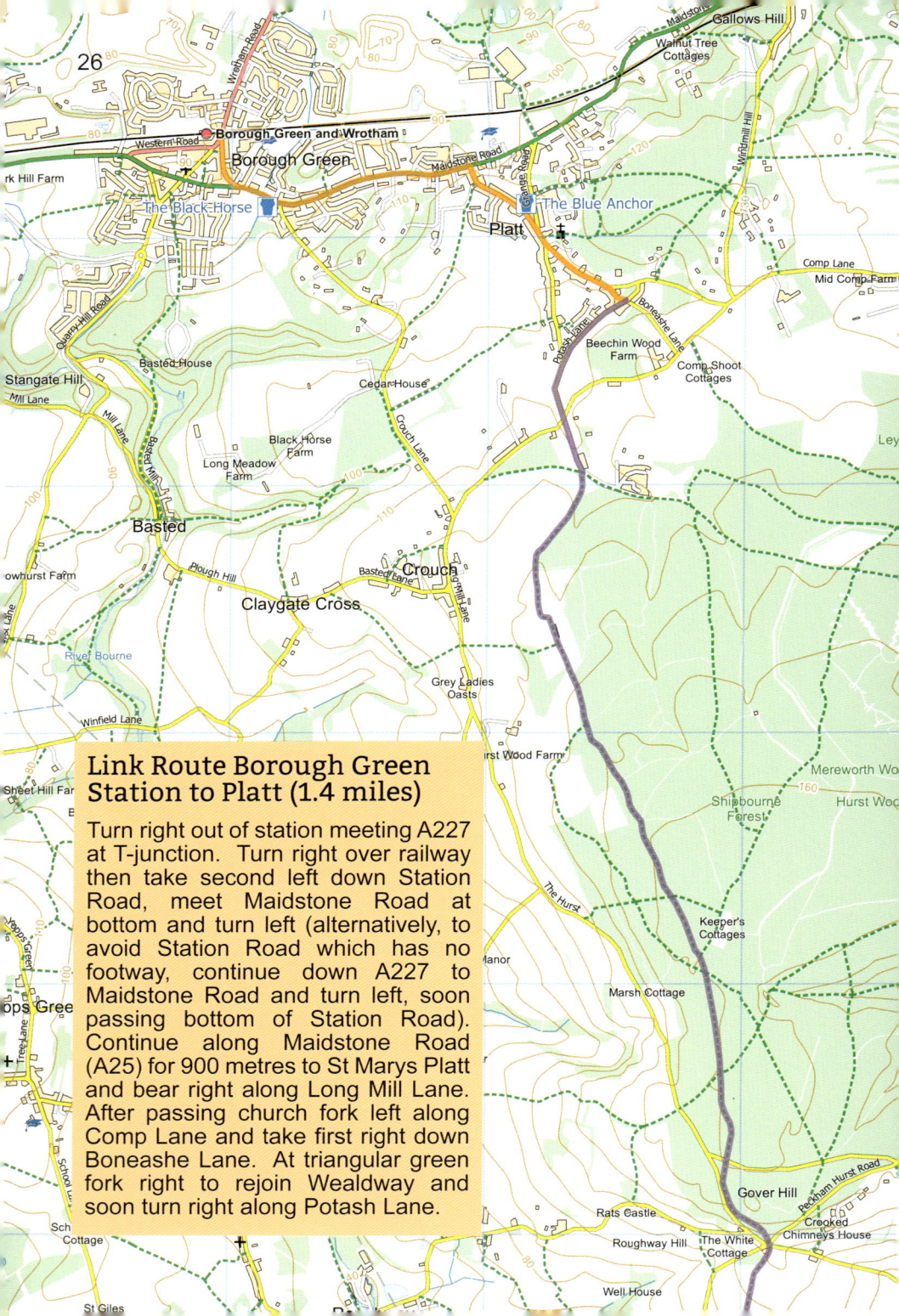

Section 3: Platt to Tonbridge (12.9 miles)

From triangular green continue along Potash Lane to meet Long Mill Lane.

Bear left and at first junction go straight ahead down lane leading to "The Old Saw Mill". At first bend, after 200 metres, where road splits and becomes private, take WW signposted byway set back to the right of the fork, just right of straight ahead, into Mereworth Woods.

Follow this path ignoring all routes off, initially heading SW but soon bearing SSE, for nearly two miles to Swanton Road.

Take narrower path opposite into chestnut coppice plantation, soon skirting road on right, to Gover Hill (could stop briefly at viewpoint) and junction of roads.

Go straight across down stony track to left of cottage for 580 metres to junction of paths. Now joining Greensand Way, turn left along bottom of orchard; at corner bear right onto track and follow to Matthews Lane at East Lodge. Turn left, bear right round bend then take path through hedge immediately on right. Go through gate then follow left hand edge of field, bearing right to opposite corner and farm track. Turn left out of field through gate, bear right and immediately turn left onto track opposite Pear Tree Cottage. At first bend go ahead through gate onto village green at West Peckham.

Cross green to right of church and go forward along Church Road (keeping church on your left) to junction with Mereworth Road in about 180 metres. Take track on right immediately after end of brick wall on right, now leaving Greensand Way.

Follow track between hedges then go straight ahead across arable field to protruding corner of hedge. Go through gap and along left hand edge of next field to corner. Go through gap and pedestrian gate then bear diagonally right across next field to corner. Bear left onto track between fence and hedge; follow to Maidstone Road.

Bear right across road to pedestrian gate, cross farm track and head diagonally across field; at the time of writing the route is marked by a clear track, half way across passing between two large arrays of polytunnels; but these will not necessarily still be in place. Go through gap in hedge and straight across grassy field, possibly with large array of polytunnels on right. At far side, turn right along track with hedge on left. Head gently downhill to pass through strip of woodland then gently up to point where track

West Peckham

turns sharp right; take track on left leading shortly to Peckham Place Farm. Turn right down farm track to Bells Farm Road. Turn left and after 90 metres turn right along track signed Little Rhoden Farm.

Follow track to and through orchard to hedge at bottom. Go over footbridge and continue straight across large field to corner of fence which protrudes from right hand field edge. Continue in same direction with fence on right to Hatches Lane. Turn right past converted oasthouses on right and at road junction turn left past Kent House Farm. Follow Pierce Mill Lane for 780 metres then, just before bridge over river Bourne, go up drive on right and through gate.

Immediately bear left along path between river on left and hedge on right soon crossing footbridge over side stream. On reaching open field, follow left hand edge to bridge over Bourne on left in about 150 metres. Cross bridge and go straight across to hedge. Bear left along hedge to corner then right down field edge (soon with stream on right) to lane at Barnes Street.

Turn right for 50 metres or so and take signed path on left down track and over stile. Turn left before fence ahead then right through gate at end of field. Follow track and then path through several gates and fields with stream on left and keep going to bridge over the Medway.

Cross bridge and turn right along river bank. At East Lock follow path over footbridge across Medway and continue along north bank with river on your left. Pass under Hartlake Bridge, pass Porter's Lock then Eldridge's Lock. Continue to outskirts of Tonbridge and bridge carrying A26. Leave river bank, turn left across bridge then right along river bank again. Pass Town Lock and at moorings bear left onto Medway Wharf Road and follow to High Street.

Turn left to reach station in about 500 metres or cross bridge and street towards information board beneath castle wall to continue along the Wealdway.

Route Planning

The full walk from Borough Green station to Tonbridge Castle at 12.8 miles may be a little on the long side for some walkers. There are various opportunities to split the route, although none is ideal.

The first is at West Peckham from where a walk of 0.8 miles along a quiet lane (but without a footway) leads to Mereworth School where buses to Maidstone and Tonbridge can be caught.

The route crosses Maidstone Road (A26) near Grove Farm. There are frequent bus services (7 and 77) between Maidstone and Tonbridge along the road but unfortunately the nearest bus stops are at Mereworth School and on the outskirts of Hadlow opposite the end of Common Road, each more than a mile away along a busy road. You could also cut across country from various places, for example Kent House Farm Oasts to catch the No 7 bus in Hadlow.

The final option is to leave the Wealdway at a junction of paths just north of Barnes Street and take the footpath to Golden Green where there are buses (service 208) to Tonbridge from a stop outside The Bell Inn.

Points of Interest

West Peckham

Cricket matches on the picturesque village green are overlooked by a 14th or 15th century church with a late Saxon tower and a traditional pub, The Swan. The church is particularly noted for its raised pew built in the 17th century for the Geary family who owned nearby Oxenhoath.

Hadlow Tower

This folly, of which there are many glimpses on this section of the walk, was originally part of a neo-Gothic castle completed in 1838 by Walter Barton May. Some say its purpose was to remind May's estranged wife of him wherever she went, some say it was to enable him to spy on her and some say it was intended to give sight of the sea but the challenge of raising it high enough proved too great. The rest of the castle was demolished in 1951 leaving the 150 ft high tower in splendid isolation. It fell into decay but early this century it was superbly restored at huge expense, partly funded by Historic England and the Heritage Lottery Fund. For a while the tower was let as very up-market holiday accommodation and, as a condition of the funding arrangements, opened occasionally to the public. Following the financial failure of the Vivat Trust which undertook the work, the tower is apparently now in private hands and it seems that the public opening obligation is not being fulfilled.

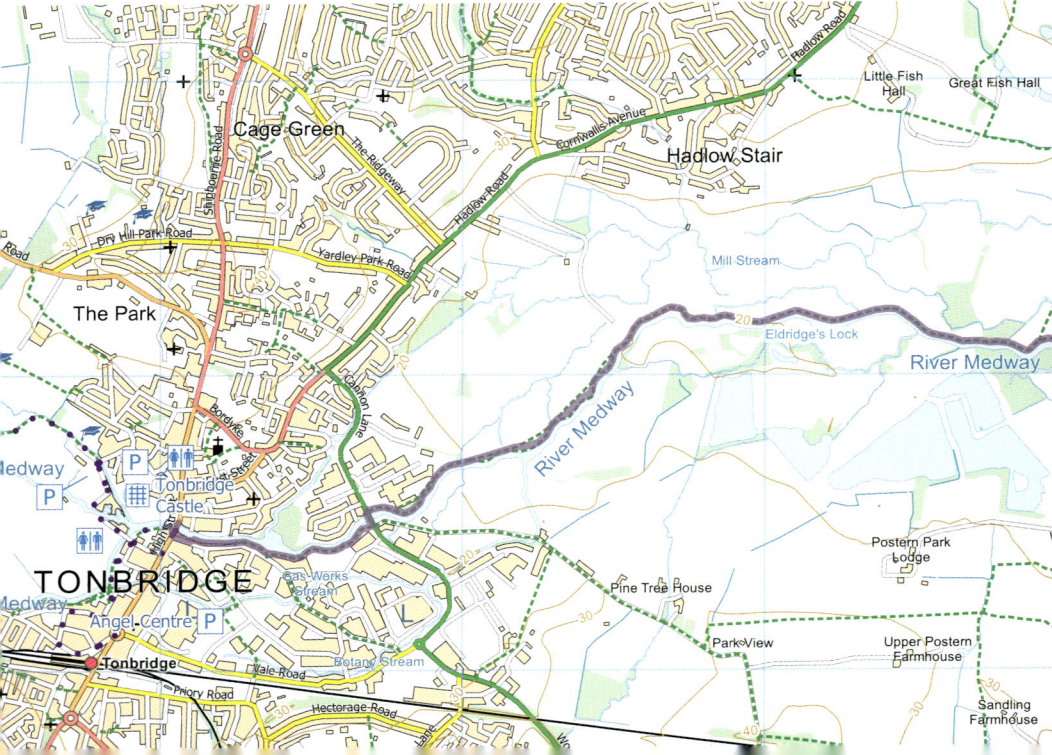

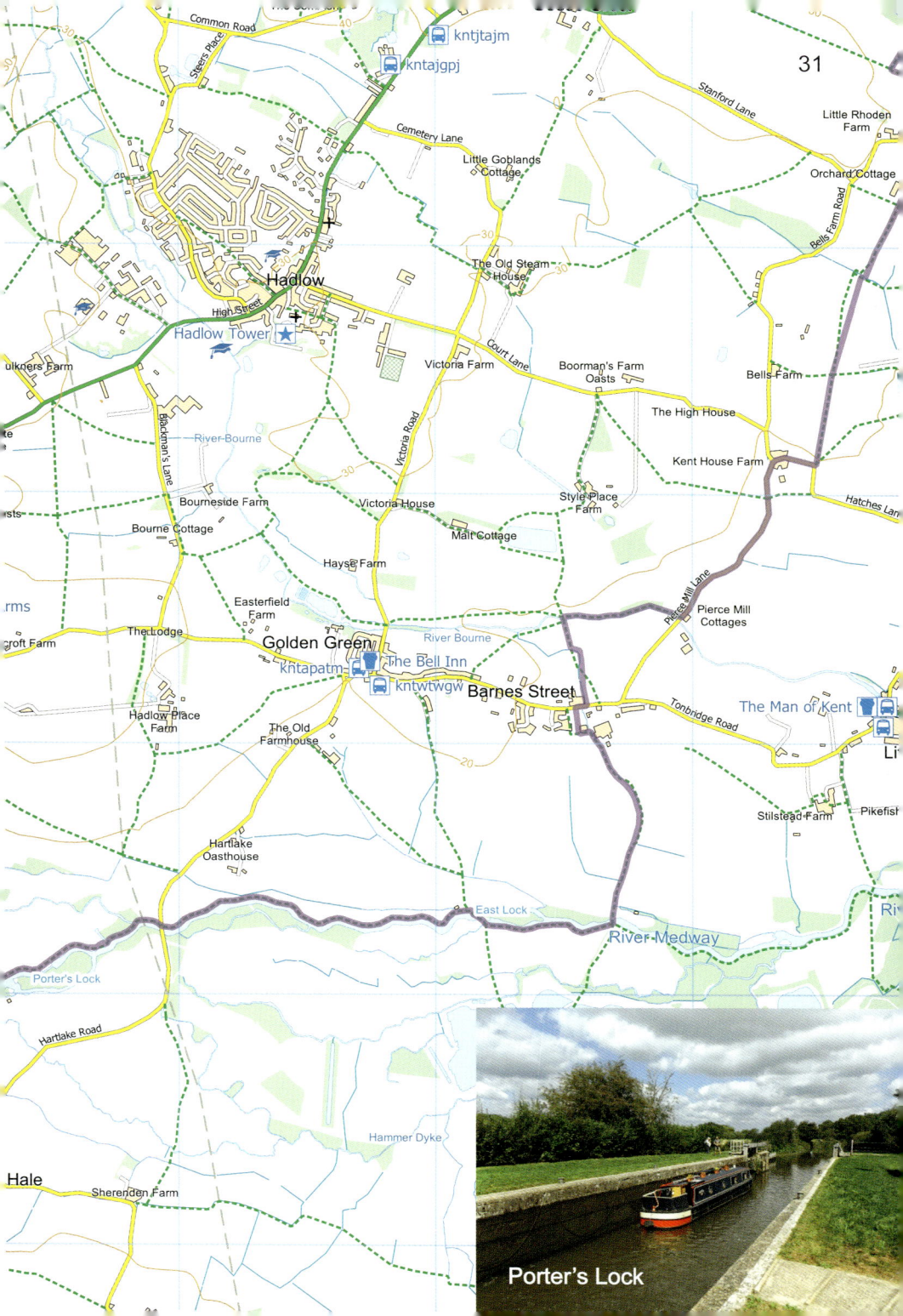

Hartlake Bridge Disaster

In October 1853 thirty hop-pickers were drowned when a wagon returning them to their camp across the bridge crashed through the wooden side into the swollen river. The coroner found that the cause of the accident was failure by the Medway Navigation Company to maintain the bridge and roadway adequately but the company refused to contribute to the cost of burying the victims in Hadlow churchyard where a monument has been erected.

Tonbridge Town Trail

Tonbridge makes much of its connections with the family of Jane Austen, many of whom were prominent citizens in the 15th century. Following the trail described here is a good way of exploring this historic town. An hour should be ample time for the trail unless you include a tour of the castle.

1. Tonbridge Castle

Tonbridge Castle

Only the 13th century gatehouse and parts of the outer walls have survived partial demolition after the Civil War and plundering for stone in the 18th century. The adjacent mansion was built in 1791 and now houses Tonbridge & Malling Borough council as well as the visitor centre. The gatehouse is open to the public and contains various exhibitions – it is one of Simon Jenkins's 1000 best houses.

2. Old Fire Station

Now an art centre and café.

3. Bank House

This surprisingly modern looking building was in fact built in 1723 as the town workhouse. It was taken over as a school in 1836 when two extra stories were added to the original two. It is now used as offices.

4. Corn Exchange

Built as a chapel for the Independent Congregationalists in 1790, the building became the Corn Exchange in 1876.

Old Fire Station

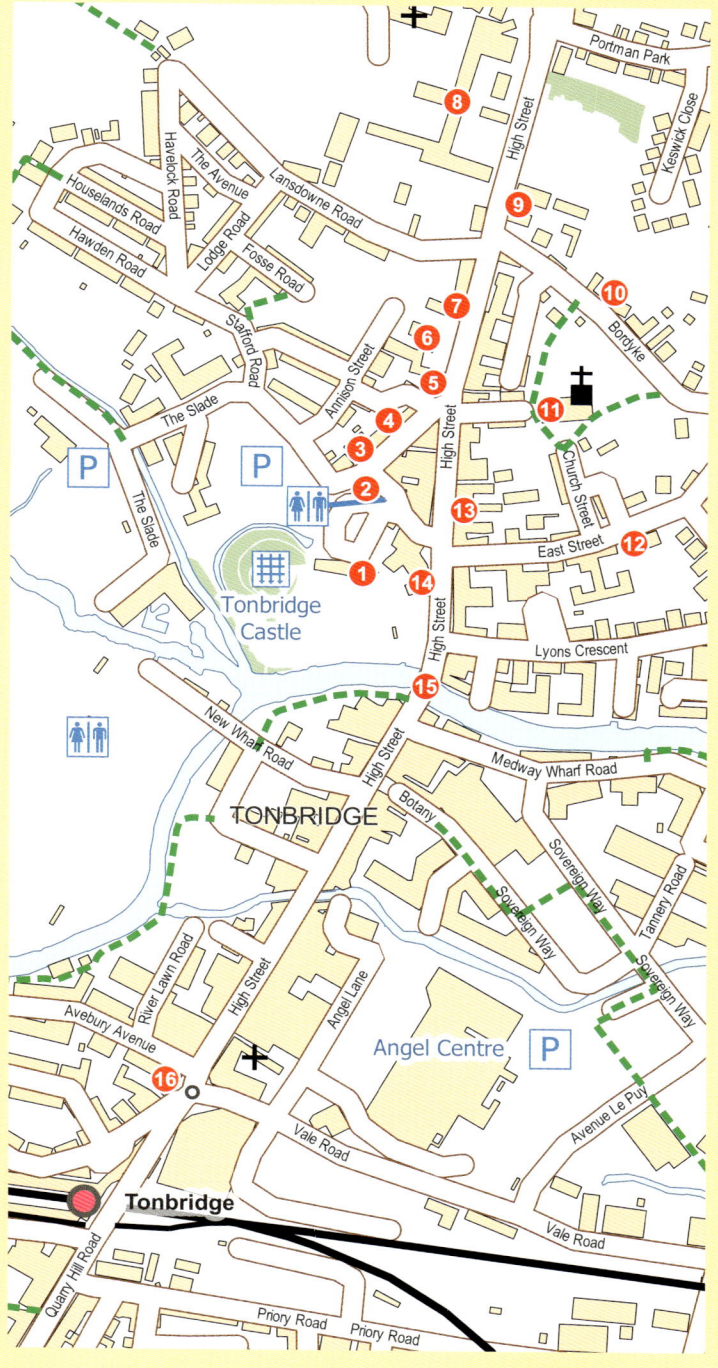

From 1910 various military units occupied the building until its conversion for commercial use, probably early in the 21st century.

5. 174 High Street

The home of William Austen, grandfather of novelist Jane Austen, may once have stood on this site.

6. 180 & 182 High Street

The Reverend George Austen, cousin of Jane Austen's father George is believed to have lived in Fosse Bank on the site of 182 High Street and to have subsequently moved next door to No 180.

7. Blair House (186 High Street)

Parts dating from 1490, the building is named after William Blair who once ran the printing press for the local paper here. It has also been the home of apothecary Thomas Austen, Jane's great uncle, a non-conformist meeting house, a boys' school and the White Hart tavern.

Port Reeve's House

8. Tonbridge School

The school was founded by Sir Andrew Judde in 1553. George Austen, Jane's father, was a pupil here and after taking a degree at Oxford returned as a master.

9. Ferox Hall

A ferox is a large trout. The hall was built in 1755 and substantially altered in 1878. Anna Atkins was born here in 1789, the daughter of John George Children who was Secretary of the Royal Society. Anna produced one of the first scientific books to be illustrated with photographs, "British Algae: Cyanotype Impressions". She used the cyanotype process which uses iron salts instead of the more expensive silver salts used by conventional photography at the time – this process continued to be used until the late 20th century for architectural plans ("blue prints"). Anna later lived and worked at Halstead Place near Orpington.

10. Chauntlers

Jane Austen's great grandmother lived here prior to her marriage to John Austen. The house has now been divided into two – the Priory and the Red House.

11. Church of St Peter and St Paul

Of the original Norman church only parts of the north wall of the chancel remain. The church was substantially altered and enlarged in 1877 by Ewan Christian, Architect to the Ecclesiastical Commissioners, who also designed the National Portrait Gallery.

12. Port Reeve's House

Chequers Inn

This 15th century timber-framed house with a sandstone base is famed for its oriel windows. The Port Reeve probably regulated and levied tolls on goods entering the town along East Street where the house stands. At one time it was divided into two cottages, one of them a sweet shop. It has also been used as the Old Swan Inn.

13. Rose & Crown

A 17th century timber-framed building is hidden behind the 18th century brick façade. It was an important coaching inn in the 18th & 19th centuries for those travelling from London to the south coast, particularly Rye. At one time a four-horse coach would stop here every half hour on weekdays.

14. Chequers Inn

Another important coaching inn, still displaying its timber frame.

15. Great Bridge

Great Bridge

There has been a bridge across the Medway here at least since 1191 and the current bridge was built in 1887 with half the cost contributed by the Rochester Bridge Trust. The bridge was widened in 1913 and again between 1925 and 1928 with contributions from the Rochester Bridge Trust on both occasions.

16. Library

The fine brick building at the corner of Avebury Avenue was built in 1890 and has housed not only the library since 1900 but also a Technical Institute and Tonbridge's first grammar school for girls. On the opposite side of the High Street is the site of the former Priory, demolished in 1842 to accommodate the station when the railway from Redhill was built. The station was moved to its present location in 1864 when the line from Sevenoaks was built.

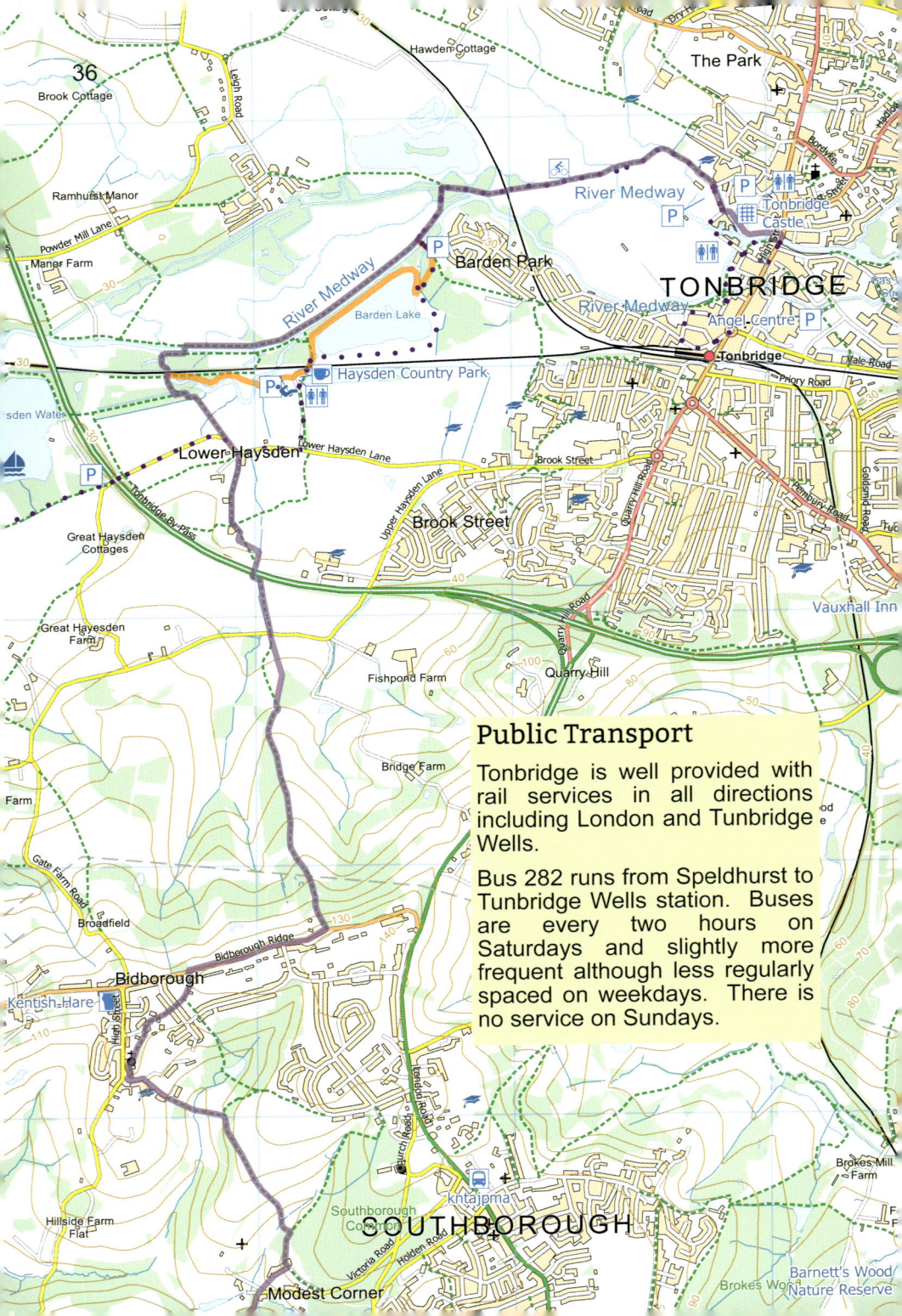

Section 4: Tonbridge to Speldhurst (6.5 miles)

From High Street take path to left of information board between Medway on left and castle walls on right. On reaching bridge on left, cross to swimming pool and turn right through car park keeping miniature railway on left. At entrance to car park take signposted asphalt path ahead adjacent to stream on right, soon with playing fields of Tonbridge School beyond. After a while the cycle track to Penshurst runs alongside and then crosses the footpath. Go under railway track, and after 250 metres at T-junction turn left over bridge still parallel to, or sharing route with, cycle track. After another 250 metres when cycle track goes left over Lucifer Bridge with fine lattice-work sides, go straight forward past information board along bank of Medway[1].

Continue for 1000 metres to first bridge (Friendship Bridge) over Medway on left, cross and turn right. Take first left turn, soon passing under railway. Go ahead into woodland, cross Straight Mile Bridge, turn left then right over Weald Way Bridge then left and right again. Follow bridleway to Lower Haysden Lane. Go ahead along lane to bend then bear right keeping row of cottages on left. Follow bridleway to Manor Farm and bear left towards oast houses then right through gate just before gateway. Follow path to end of fence on left then bear left to corner of meadow. Turn right along path through subway under A21.

On far side bear left over stile and footbridge then sharp right along right hand field edge to cross footbridge. Bear left across Upper Haysden Lane and take path up field towards protruding corner of wood then along field edge with wood on left to corner. Go through gap to next field and follow right hand edge to gate at top corner then follow steep path up through wood to road (Bidborough Ridge, B2176).

Turn right along road for 570 metres then take fenced path on left between houses (just after number 67). Ignore left turn, cross Woodland Way, cross cul-de-sac and take path on left towards recreation ground. At fork keep right and follow to Bidborough churchyard.

Pass church, go down steps to lych gate, turn left along Spring Lane passing school on your right. Follow lane as it bears right downhill. At bottom go straight ahead along downhill path. On entering meadow head uphill alongside hedge to wood at top, through kissing gate, then bear right diagonally uphill along path through wood. Emerging into meadow, continue in same line bearing half right to gate at protruding corner of Southborough Cemetery. Follow cemetery hedge on right down to steps and cross footbridge. On far side head up to T-junction and turn right, soon emerging at Modest Corner.

Turn right down street and at bottom follow path down across cemetery drive to road (Bentham Hill). Bear right uphill (beware of traffic) and at junction with Stockland Green Road continue forward for 300 metres. Just opposite first house on right, take path on left (just after Birchetts

---

[1] This path can be horribly muddy after rain when, unless you are a purist for following the official route, you might prefer the alternative via the toilets and refreshment kiosk shown in orange on the map. This will return you to the official route just south of the railway, so turn left towards Straight Mile Bridge and continue as above.

Cottage) between fences then along left hand edge of field still between fences to stile. Follow left hand edge of second field, turn right at corner along hedge and at corner go through gate and along path between fences down to Stockland Green Road.

Turn right for 75 metres and take path on left across yard at Forge House downhill to stream. Cross and go up track past former water mill on left continuing to Speldhurst Hill. Cross to pavement, turn right up to junction and cross to brick footway at top. Turn left and soon reach steps offering a detour to Speldhurst Church where there are benches outside and Burne-Jones windows inside.

Two fine listed buildings at Lower Haysden viewed from the Wealdway

Points of Interest

Haysden Country Park

The 161-acre site includes Haysden Water and Barden Lake, both the result of gravel extraction. There are toilets and a refreshment kiosk but you would have to take a route through the park other than the Wealdway in order to pass them – a suggested route is shown in orange on the map. The cycle route from Tonbridge to Penshurst passes through the park. There is a detailed map on pages 42-43.

Haysden Country Park

Lucifer Bridge

Apparently the name arose because during a dispute between locals and the landowner in the early 18th century someone scrawled "How though art fallen from heaven, O Lucifer" on the bridge.

Bidborough

The village sits on the south side of the road that runs along an east-west oriented sandstone ridge. The north side of the ridge falls away steeply – you probably noticed as you climbed up – offering fine views across the Medway valley to the Greensand ridge. The old village is on the south side with its small but prominent sandstone church boasting both Saxon and Norman features and offering fine views along the ridge and south into the Weald.

The splendid view from the churchyard includes, in addition to the fine Wealden countryside, a windmill and a Victorian country house once known as Elm Court but now called Bidborough Court.

The **windmill** has been unused since about 1900 when it was struck by lightning, two sweeps fell and there was insufficient trade to justify the cost of repair.

Bidborough Court is described as "ambitious" in its Historic England Grade II listing. It was built around 1860 and has been the residence of a member of Lloyds, a war-time hospital and part of a school. Now it is divided into apartments.

Bidborough Church

In the 20th century the village expanded to the south east, almost merging with Southborough, with the building of a housing estate on what had once been the estate of Great Bounds with a history dating back to Edward I and in the 17th century the home of Dorothy Spencer, Countess of Sunderland, after her second marriage to Sir Robert Smythe who owned the estate.

Modest Corner

The name may derive from 14th century resident John Mode. A spring here was the source for one of Kent's earliest water supply undertakings established in 1885 by Southborough Urban District Council.

Former Beehive Pub

As you descend the hill you will pass the white weatherboarded former Beehive pub on your right. Until 1857 it was two cottages, then converted into a brewery and becoming an inn in 1873. It was converted to a single dwelling in 1997.

Speldhurst Mill

Also known as Taylor's Mill, this is one of Kent's best preserved water powered corn mills. The wheel, which was originally driven by water pouring into buckets attached to it, can still be seen although it has deteriorated significantly in the last decade and it is not certain what its fate will be following a redevelopment of the site as residential accommodation that is taking place at the time of writing. The mill pond is still intact and full of water.

Speldhurst

The parish of Speldhurst is one of the oldest hereabouts and was once larger, encompassing much land that is now in surrounding parishes. The present church was built on the site of several predecessors. The medieval church was struck by lightning and destroyed in 1791. Its replacement was of poor quality and had to be demolished in 1870. The present church was built by John Oldrid Scott, son of George Gilbert Scott who championed the Gothic revival, and there is a notable series of windows by the Pre-Raphaelite artist Edward Burne-Jones.

Speldhurst Churchyard

While opinions vary on the merits of the church building, its location is indisputably splendid at the edge of a sandstone plateau and from its door one sees nothing but fine ancient buildings including, across the road, a picturesque old inn, the George and Dragon.

The village has a thriving community shop and post office, set up in 2019 when the proprietor of its predecessor retired and the village seemed likely to be left without a shop.

George & Dragon

The pub's website claims that the building dates from 1212. However, its Grade II* listing with Historic England says it is a late medieval hall house, probably from the late 15th century with major late 16th and early 17th century improvements. Either way it has been a pub for over 200 years and has many exposed timbers from its oak frame.

George & Dragon, Speldhurst

Tunbridge Wells Circular Walk

Between Modest Corner and Bullingstone (on the next section of the walk) the route of the Wealdway largely overlaps with that of the Tunbridge Wells Circular Walk, a 27.5 mile route encircling the town with link routes to the town centre to facilitate access by public transport. Kent Ramblers have published a guide to the walk which also includes descriptions of a Tunbridge Wells town trail and six walks in the High Weald around the market town of Cranbrook.

The panel below is taken from a planned information board for Groombridge car park

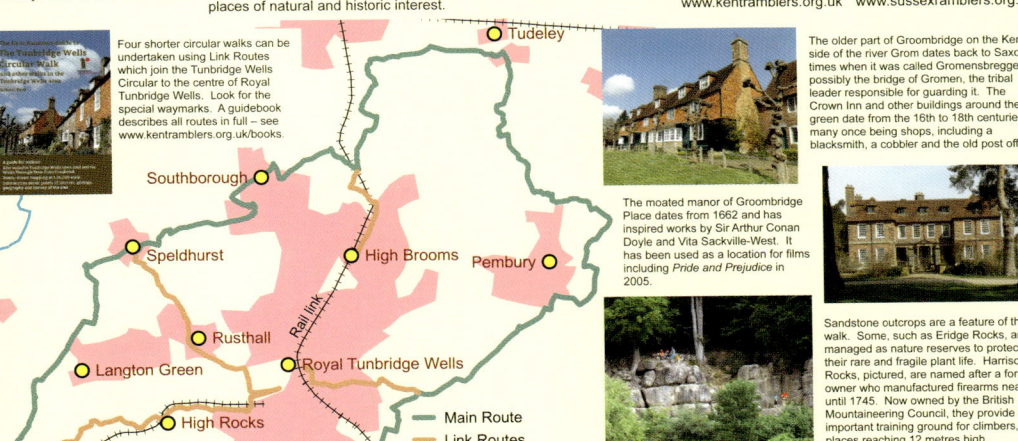

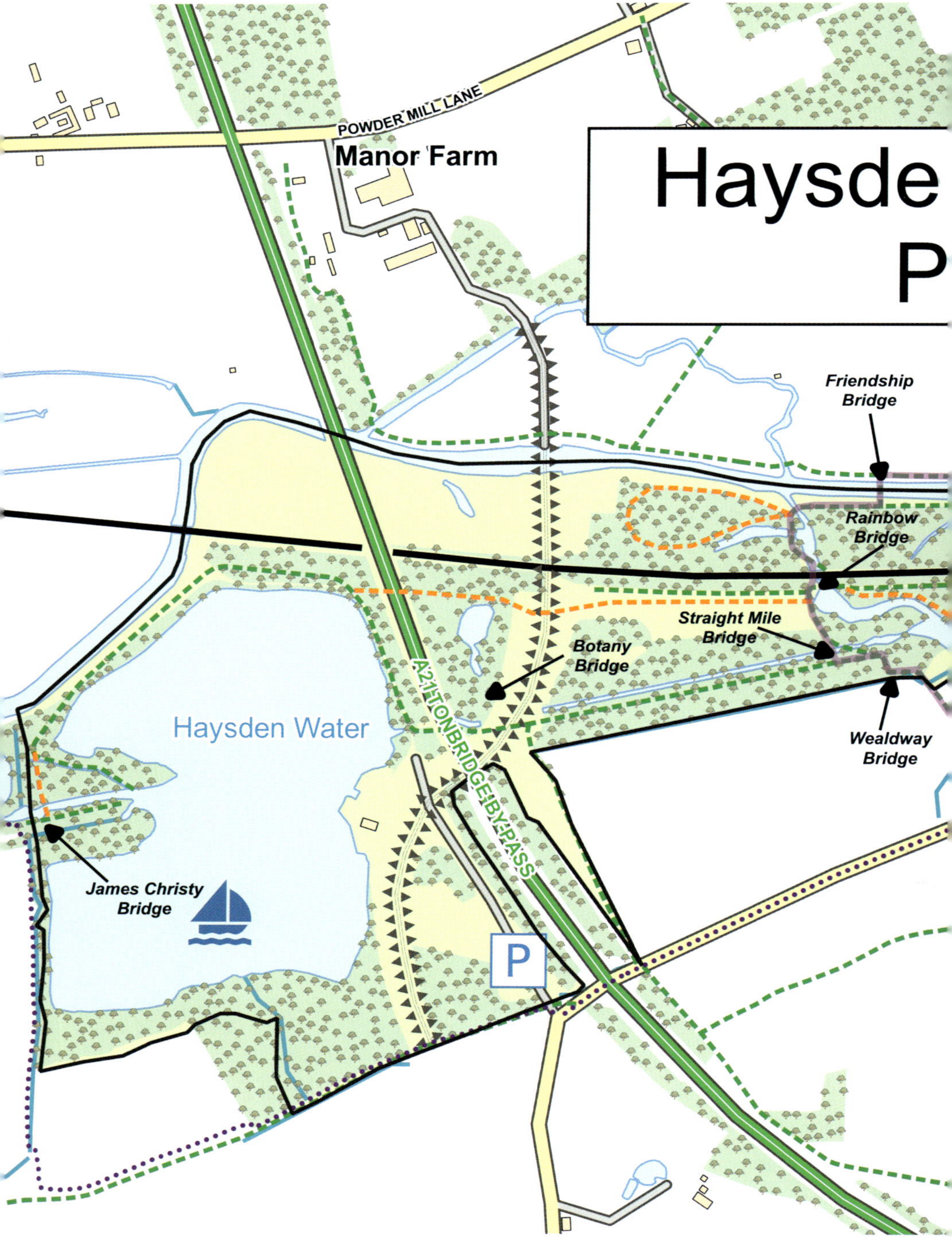

POWDER MILL LANE

Manor Farm

Haysde
P

Friendship Bridge

Rainbow Bridge

Straight Mile Bridge

Botany Bridge

Wealdway Bridge

Haysden Water

A21 TONBRIDGE BYPASS

James Christy Bridge

P

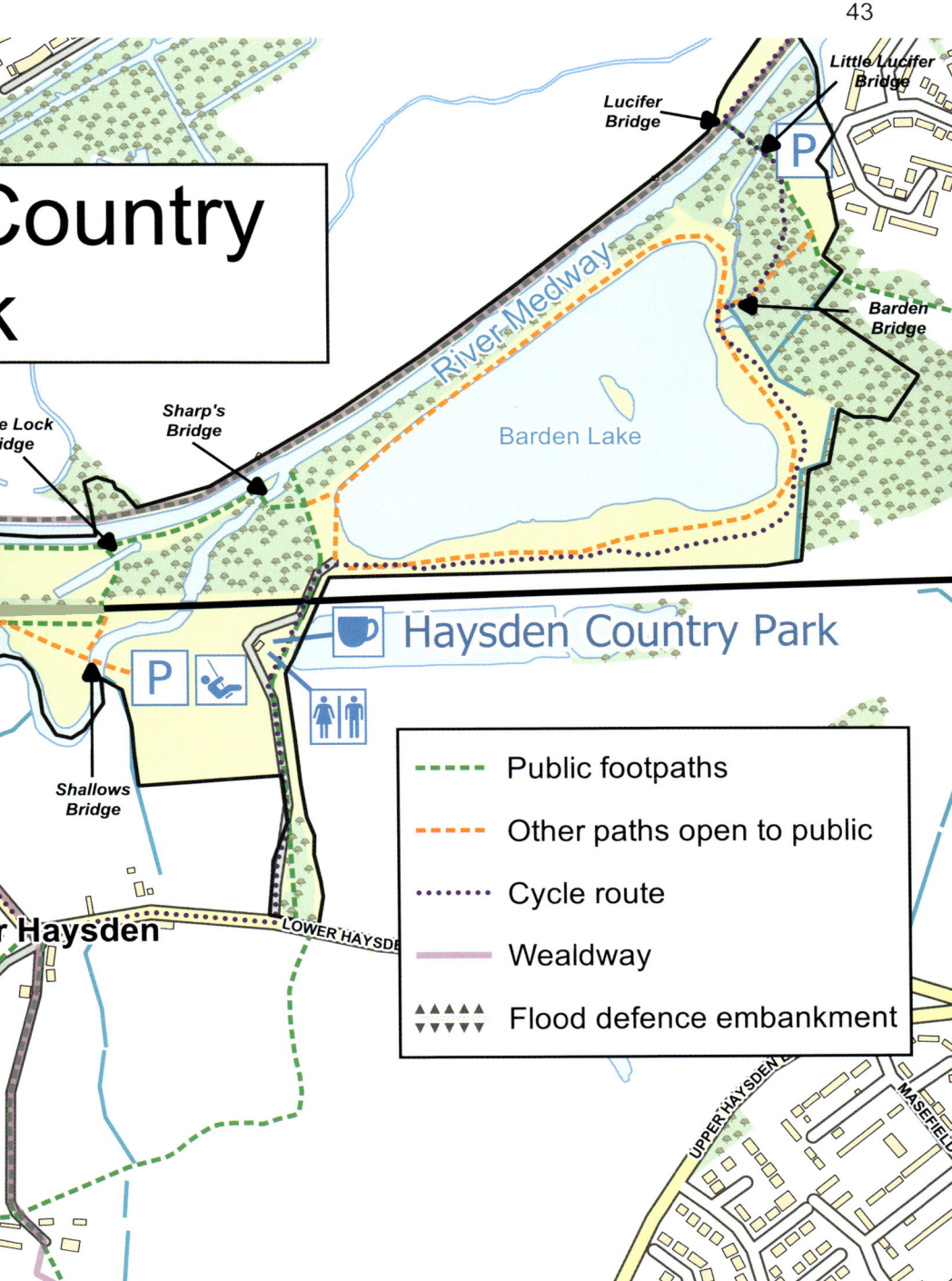

Section 5: Speldhurst to Withyham (6.5 miles)

Leaving the churchyard through the lych gate, follow Penshurst Road round to right (ignoring first path on left after 70 metres) and after 150 metres take path on left through old iron gate, signposted to Bullingstone. Go forward between houses then along fenced path between fields down to Bullingstone Lane.

Turn right for 100 metres then take path on left (just after Holly Cottage) between houses. On entering wood at junction of paths bear right, soon descending to wooden footbridge. Cross and continue through wood, soon bearing left and climbing gradually to top edge of wood. Emerge in field and head diagonally across to kissing gate. Continue in same direction to corner of next field then between ponds to junction of lanes.

Turn left along Old House Lane, ignoring The Lane on right, to first turn on left (Leggs' Lane). Take path on right up bank, initially alongside fence then past pond and along left hand edge of field to join The Lane. Turn left and follow lane all the way to Fordcombe.

Go straight across road (B2188) to left of the new village hall and head for far left corner of playing field. Take left hand path, soon between fence and hedges, then along left hand edges of three fields. Go over stile onto track in front of houses, turn right to Broad Lane then left to A264, Ashurst Road, at Stone Cross.

Cross very carefully and turn left along verge to bend then take path on right through kissing gate to right of gate across private drive. Follow path along backs of buildings then up steps and alongside field. Go through short section of path between hedges and walk full length of long narrow field to gate with outstanding views across Withyham valley.

Cross large field, neither climbing nor descending much but getting fine views of surrounding countryside. At far side of field make for gate some way down from top (ignore path going to top right hand corner) and go through (or use stile to right). Follow hedge/fence on the right until there is a gate leading through it; through gate turn left and follow same hedge now on your left and into meadow at bottom.

Bear slightly right across meadow to where it extends downhill and go under railway. Bear left towards large oak and make for footbridge just to right. Bear right across field to junction of paths by bridge over river Grom. Turn right across bridge and follow clear path and line of telegraph poles to second bridge, this time over Medway.

Cross field to footbridge but don't go over; instead bear left along right hand edge of field. Cross bridge into second field and at end go forward

View of Withyham Valley

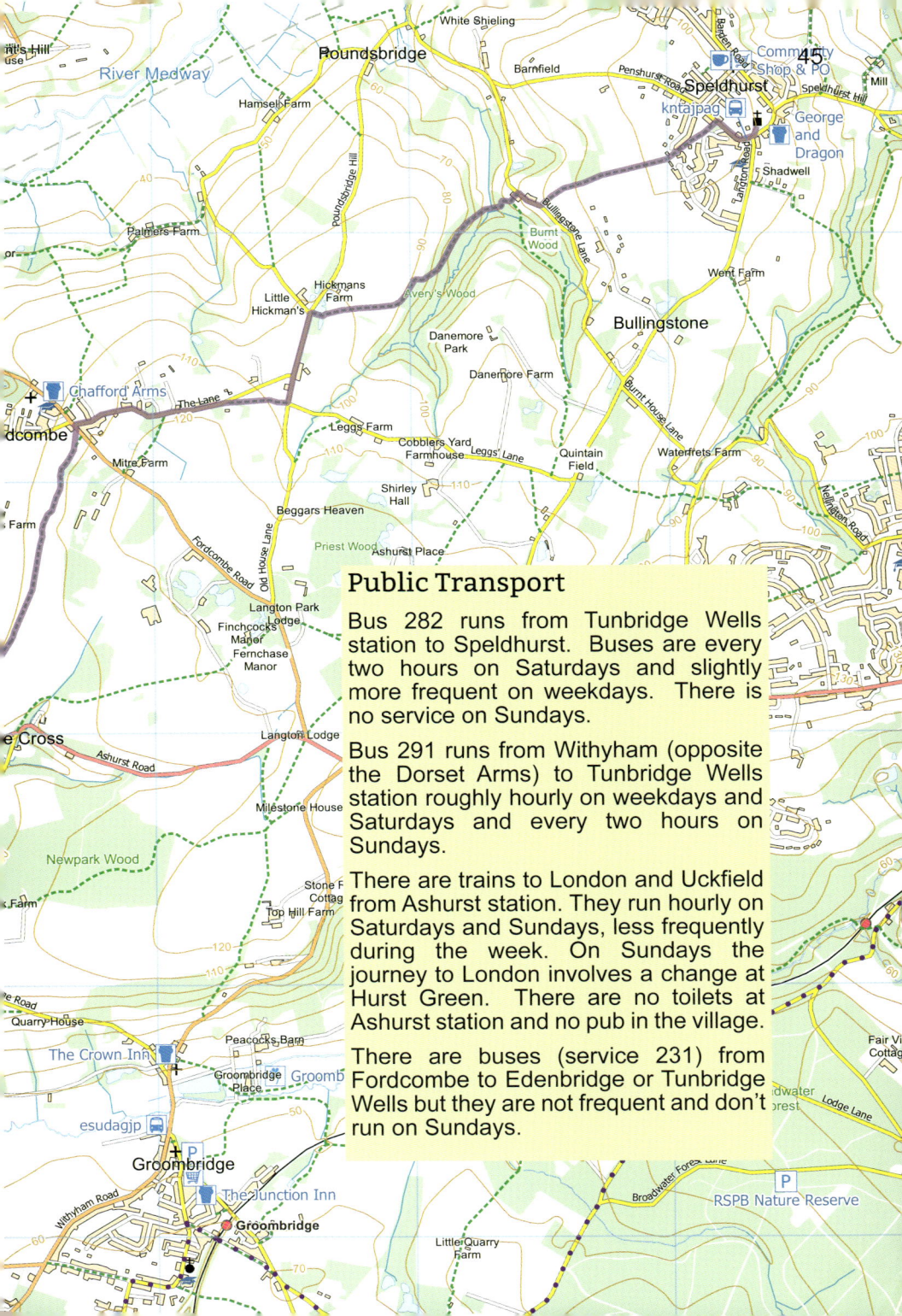

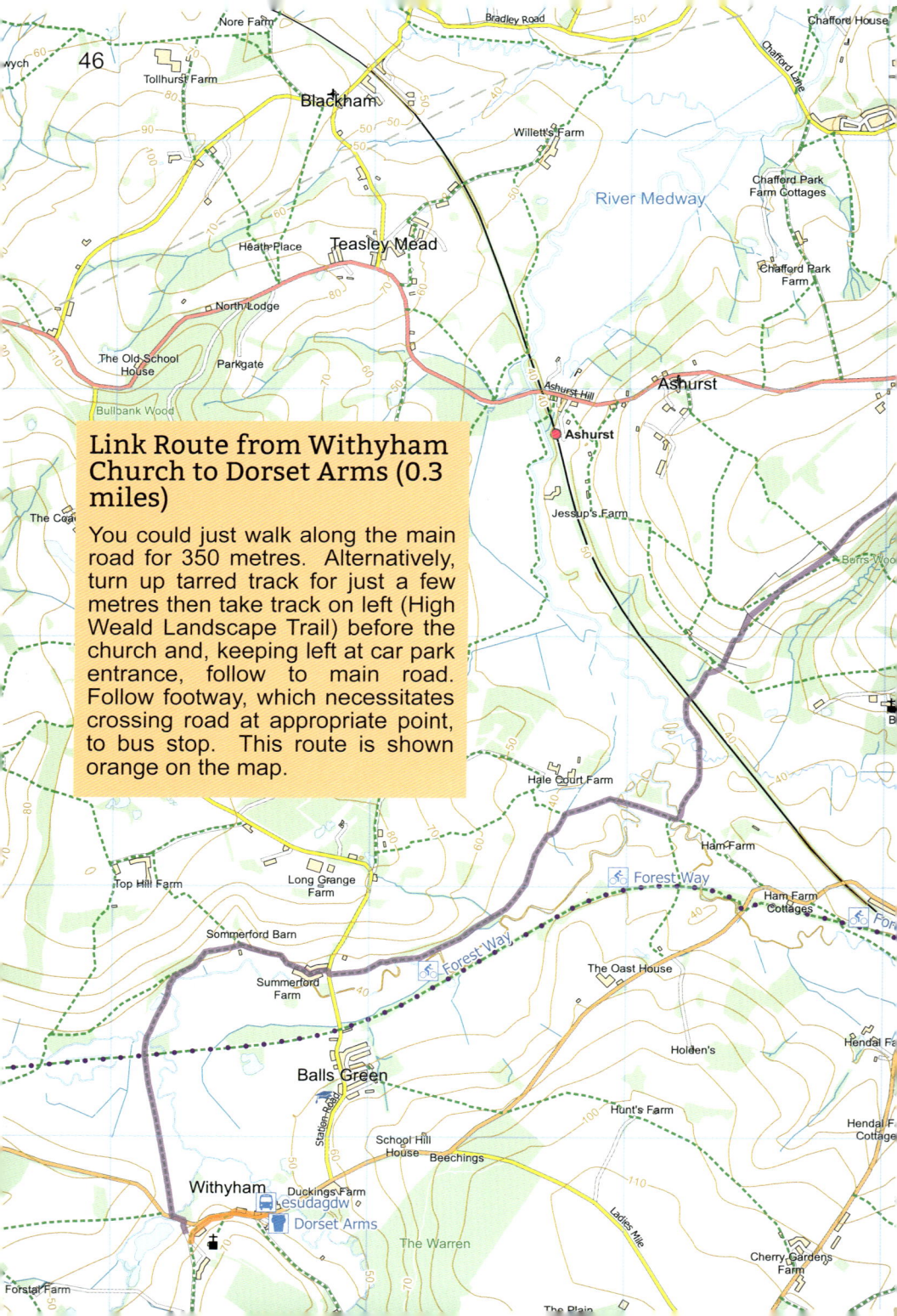

into woodland soon crossing footbridge and bearing left over second bridge. Bear right along right hand edge of pasture to Beech Green Lane.

Bear right across lane and take tarred drive through Summerford Farm. At triple oast bear right along tarred track. At end go through gate on right and turn left along grassy track between hedges. After 140 metres bear left down steps and continue on path between fences into woodland. When path divides turn left to descend steeply (take care) towards river[1]. Emerging into open pasture head for footbridge over Medway and on other side bear left to cross Forest Way (watch out for cyclists). Head straight across two large fields of grass to Withyham Road (B2110).

Turn left over bridge and almost immediately turn right up tarred track signed Withyham Parish Church.

---

[1] *Erosion of the bank of the Medway is currently threatening this section of path and there are plans for a short diversion. Once that is in place, please follow new signage.*

Between Fordcombe and Stone Cross

Points of Interest

Bullingstone

Bullingstone

There are many listed 15th and 16th century houses spaced along Bullingstone Lane. Presumably the name derives from its earliest recorded inhabitant, a farmer called Baluinch in 1218. As you leave the tiny hamlet, you part way with the Tunbridge Wells Circular Walk.

Burnt Wood and Avery's Wood

Here you walk through a typical Wealden ghyll with steeply wooded sides. You may spot orchids, wood valerian and golden saxifrage but most spectacular are the displays of bluebells each spring.

Fordcombe

The village is small but there are a pub, a school and a church. The economy was largely agricultural until 1756 when the corn mill on the Medway west of the village was converted to the production of paper and the workforce

Oasts at Summerford

greatly increased. Apparently a spring supplied water of exceptional quality that resulted in paper much in demand for banknotes, stamps and official documents because it was thought to be less palatable to ants than standard paper. The mill was bought by Wiggins Teape in 1913 and closed, the machinery being transferred to a Dover mill. There is not much to see now apart from the mill race and the foundations.

The foundation stone of the church was laid in 1848 by Henry, 1st Viscount Hardinge, who had been Governor-General of India for four years and had retired to nearby South Park (on the road from Penshurst to Fordcombe). The church was apparently completed in just nine months and seven years later Hardinge, who had met £1,000 of the £2,508 building costs, was interred in the finest tomb in the churchyard.

River Medway

The Wealdway crosses the Medway seven times, two of them on this section of the walk. Although we are here a long way from the Medway estuary, it is already a mature river meandering through a wide flood plain.

Summerford

The name means exactly what it says – before the bridge was built there was a ford that was only usable in summer when the Medway was low.

Forest Way

The Forest Way is designated as a Country Park, based around a 10 mile stretch of disused railway line from East Grinstead to Groombridge. The railway line opened in 1866 and closed in 1966 as part of the Beeching cuts. The route is part of the National Cycle Network but wide enough for walkers and equestrians too.

Designated Landscapes

There are 44 areas in England that enjoy additional statutory protection from unsuitable development – 10 National Parks and 34 Areas of Outstanding Natural Beauty (AONBs). The Wealdway crosses three of them (see map on back cover):

- Kent Downs AONB (www.kentdowns.org.uk)
- High Weald AONB (www.highweald.org)
- South Downs National Park (www.southdowns.gov.uk)

The primary purpose of designation is to conserve and enhance natural beauty but other purposes include support for farming and forestry and the promotion of understanding and enjoyment of the area's special qualities. Kent and Sussex Ramblers meet regularly with staff at the High Weald AONB unit to consider how we might support the last of these and we hope that this book will make a significant contribution. We also work together to organise the High Weald Walking Festival each autumn.

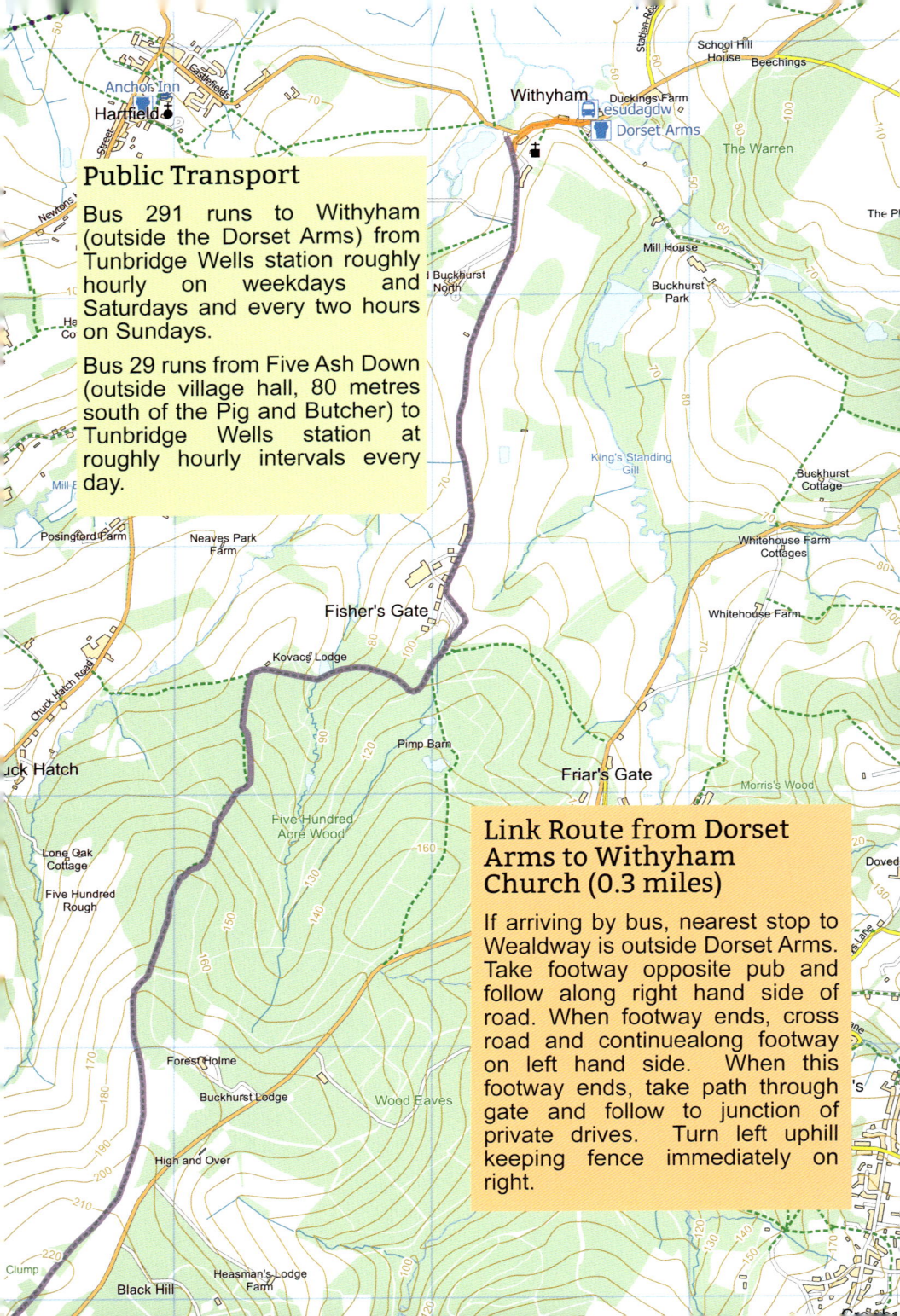

Section 6: Withyham to Five Ash Down (9.1 miles)

Thirty metres east of bridge over stream take tarred private drive uphill past church on left and adjacent to fence on right. Follow track for nearly 1.2 miles to Fisher's Gate passing several buildings on right and when track forks into two gated drives take path over stile on left into open pasture. Follow fence on right, cross stile and soon rejoin tarred drive on right. Bear left and at junction go straight ahead to meet another drive. Turn right and soon after Honeywood House take right hand fork continuing along tarred road.

After 130 metres follow road round to right and continue for a further 700 metres downhill to valley bottom. Pass entrance to Kovacs Lodge and take track uphill alongside fence. After some 200 metres, as track levels out, turn left past metal barrier and follow path, soon rising again and climbing steadily through Five Hundred Acre Wood. On meeting track coming up from right and going off to left, go forward uphill past fallen gate. Continue to climb and as path reaches edge of wood fork right, initially following edge of wood on left but soon crossing open heathland between rows of gorse bushes.[1] On reaching clump of Scots pines ahead, bear left through clump onto another wide track and turn right along it, gradually ascending, and at fork keep right (very nearly straight ahead). Pass Greenwood Gate Clump on right. Cross wide track and soon reach High Road, B2026. Cross to small car park (Lodge).

Go through car park and take path on far side, soon emerging through gate onto broad track. Follow track straight ahead (not the one going downhill to right), soon descending gradually but later climbing more steeply towards Camp Hill, a fairly prominent clump of trees on a knoll where there are seats and fine views.

Immediately past Camp Hill, turn sharp left and take path passing left of trig point down to road, B2026, at junction with New Road.

Bear straight across junction (care!) to take path over stile on south side of New Road. Follow path roughly parallel with road on left, soon crossing stile and footbridge almost back to road. Bear right along track through gorse and bracken to junction with stony track. Bear right along track, quickly turning left along ridge with fine views of South Downs on right. When track turns sharp right downhill, take path on left over stile and into wood. Meet asphalt track, bear right along it for a few metres, then take path on right briefly leaving track then crossing it again. Continue on path descending through wood ignoring all turns until across footbridge you reach clearing with small group of cottages (Glenwood House). Pass cottages and continue along track back into wood then take

---

[1] *The current OS Explorer map shows a slightly different route from here to the road but the description here fits the waymarks and paths on the ground.*

A glimpse of Buckhurst Park

View from near Camp Hill Clump

first path on right climbing to cross another track and continue through wood. On reaching broad track bear left and after 110 metres, as track begins to bear left, bear right on path descending through heather to top edge of birch wood. Turn left, soon entering wood, continue along waymarked track for 260 metres and go straight across broad track immediately after multi-fingered post. After another 280 metres meet lane and turn right along it to junction, with gates to Oldlands Hall on left.

Turn right downhill along Oldlands Hill (here signed "The Street"). After 325 metres, as road bends right at entrance to Fairwarp QEII sports field on left, bear left on track that gradually diverges from the road. Soon after joining broader track turn left through gate (rotted and fallen at time of writing) and follow path slightly right to second gate into Brickfield Meadow Nature Reserve. Cross to diagonally opposite corner, go through gate, turn left across bridge and then half-right

Gorse on Ashdown Forest with the South Downs beckoning on the horizon

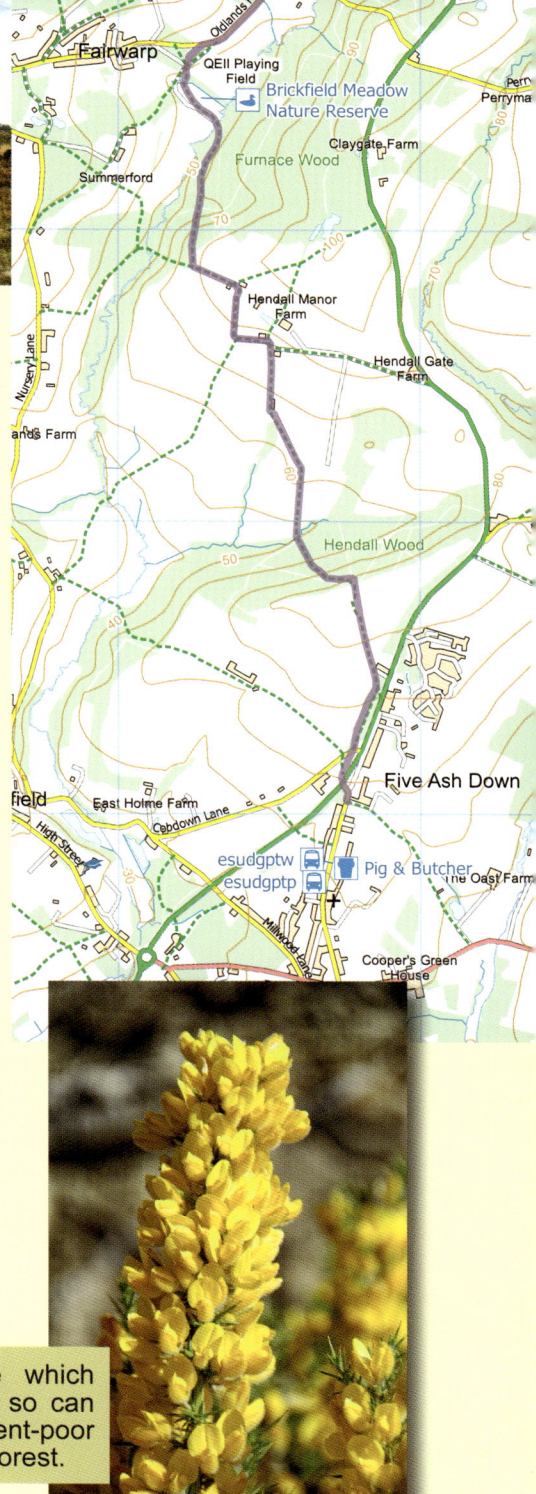

along rising forest track. On meeting broad track go straight across up steep path with steps. Follow path round to right, climbing towards edge of woodland. Just before path starts to bear right and descend, take path on left through outcrop of Ardingly Sandstone, possibly an old quarry, and follow zigzag path up to gate into field.

Head towards farm buildings at Hendall Manor, pass just to right of large barn and turn right along tarred farm track. Follow track past gate, turn left at corner (ignoring path immediately right) and after 75 metres at T-junction turn right then right again along rougher track. Just past large barn, bear left across rough ground to corner then continue along path between fences. At end take path over footbridge into wood, bearing gradually left uphill. Emerging from wood go straight across field alongside fence, through band of trees to track by house and keep right along permissive path through woodland parallel to main road (A26). Ignore any side paths to cross Cobdown Lane and follow path to A26.

Cross carefully into Five Ash Down. The bus stops are down the main street near the Pig & Butcher pub. The Wealdway continues 50 metres down the main street from the A26, left between buildings of used vehicle centre.

Gorse, a legume which fixes nitrogen and so can thrive on the nutrient-poor soils of Ashdown Forest.

Points of Interest

Withyham Church

The church of St Michael and All Angels occupies a superb position with fine views across the Weald. The original church was largely destroyed by a lightning strike in 1663 and rebuilt in 1672-80. In the 19th century the church was enlarged, its north aisle removed and the south arcade added. Internally the Sackville chapel is of particular interest and on the chancel arch is a mural painted in the mid-19th century by the then rector Reginald Sackville-West.

Withyham Church

Also in the mid-19th century, a set of 14th century paintings by Niccolò di Pietro Gerini depicting the Passion of Christ was donated to the church. Their significance and value was only recognised during restoration work in the 1990s and in 2012 they were sold for £950,000 to provide a maintenance fund for the church. Photographic reproductions are now in place.

Perhaps the most important feature is the footpath that leads from a gate at the back of the churchyard, across a field and down to the main road. This path was established in 2010 following a campaign by Sussex Ramblers leading to a public inquiry as the landowner refused to recognise the right of way.

High Weald Landscape Trail

For the few hundred metres after you pass Withyham Church, the Wealdway coincides with the High Weald Landscape Trail. While the Wealdway crosses the Weald from north to south, the HWLT crosses from Horsham in the west to Rye in the east, a total distance of 90 miles. It is superb, perhaps the best of the South East's long distance walks.

Old Buckhurst

Soon after leaving Withyham church, at a point where a path on the right takes the High Weald Landscape Trail towards Hartfield, across the field in the direction taken by the HWLT you may glimpse a stone tower poking through the trees that is the last surviving remnant of Buckhurst, abandoned in 1603 by its Sackville occupants when they moved to Knole which also lay on their vast estate.

"Thatchers" on the track to Fisher's G

Buckhurst Park

Following a dispute over a will, the Sackville estate was split between two branches of the family, one retaining Knole and the other taking Buckhurst. Here they built a new house, originally called Stoneland Lodge, but later renamed Buckhurst Park, that you can see in the distance on your left as you approach Fisher's Gate, particularly as you climb the stile when leaving the asphalt drive. The house was substantially enlarged in the mid-18th century and remodelled again in the early 19th century in the Elizabethan style. In 1903 while the house was let to tenant R H Benson additions designed by Edwin Lutyens were made but demolished in the 1950s. The surrounding parkland was landscaped in 1830-35 by Humphrey Repton. The High Weald Landscape Trail passes through the parkland giving good views of two lakes but not of the house. The garden, which cannot be seen, was apparently designed by Lutyens with planting advice from Gertrude Jekyll (1843-1932).

Fisher's Gate

Originally named Fidges Gate, here was one of the original gates (some are referred to as "hatches") into Royal Ashdown Forest. One source suggests that "Fidges" is derived from "Firchett", meaning polecat, while another suggests it is derived from the name of its original owner in 1327, Richard Fychet. The latter source also suggests that the garden of the main house, said in a booklet dated 1959 to be black and white and dating from the twelfth century, yet curiously not a listed building, may have been designed by Gertrude Jekyll.

Five Hundred Acre Wood

This wood inspired the Hundred Aker Wood in the Winnie-the-Pooh books by A A Milne who lived at nearby Cotchford Farm. Not far away is Pooh Sticks Bridge where Pooh and Piglet would drop sticks into the river upstream and then argue about whose stick had emerged first on the downstream side.

Old Lodge Nature Reserve

The entrance to the reserve is only a couple of minutes' walk to your right as you cross High Road (B2026). The quite large reserve is owned and run by Sussex Wildlife Trust. Admission is free but the car park belongs to the Conservators of Ashdown Forest who charge for parking. The altitude of the reserve gives it a cooler climate which attracts species such as the redstart which are more commonly found in the north and west of the UK and are otherwise rare in Sussex. The reserve has an open landscape of heather and grass with clumps of gorse and scattered birches and oaks.

Kings Standing

The Wealdway passes a couple of hundred metres to the west of Kings Standing, the highest point on Ashdown Forest. There is a small rectangle of Scot pines planted in 1816 in a pre-existing banked enclosure. On old maps it is marked as "King James's Standing". Modern Ordnance Survey maps bear the label "Pillow Mound" which usually indicates a stone mound covered in earth as an artificial rabbit warren. In medieval times rabbits were carefully nurtured for their meat and fur. There is a car park in which an ice cream van is often to be found.

Roman Road

The London to Lewes Roman road ran across Ashdown forest and the Wealdway runs quite closely parallel to it from the top of Five Hundred Acre Wood to Camp Hill, passing very close to the point where Roman Road car park is now situated. It was probably built in the later first or early second century to link London and Lewes with the iron works of the Weald.

Camp Hill

Here the Wealdway was opened on 27 September 1981 by the Chairman of the Countryside Commission, attended by some 500 delegates from Britain and fourteen European walking organisations. Although lower than Kings Standing, Camp Hill offers more extensive views across Ashdown Forest.

Oldlands Hall

The house, now divided into several dwellings, was built from 1869 by the antiquary Alexander Nesbitt. The park and gardens were developed by accomplished gardener Edward Luckhurst. In 1920 the estate was sold to Frederick Eckstein, and later passed to his son Sir Bernard. Following the latter's death, in 1948 the estate was broken up and the house divided into several dwellings.

The estate contains evidence of both the Roman and Tudor iron industries.

Hendall Manor

The manor house was built in the 16th century and refaced in the 19th. It was owned by the Pope family who are said to have been lawyers, landowners and iron entrepreneurs. They owned and built Hendall furnace which was let to ironmaster Ralphe Hogge – of whom more on the next section of the walk.

The furnace was in the valley bottom in Furnace Wood through which the Wealdway passed before emerging to approach Hendall Manor. There was a pond to drive the furnace bellows but this is now dry. It is thought that there might later have been a forge here too.

Ashdown Forest

The Ashdown beds are the oldest of the Wealden rocks and accordingly they occur in the central and highest part of the Weald. They produce sandy soils from which most nutrients have been leached and so are poorly suited to agriculture, supporting mainly heathland and woodland.

This is the largest and best-preserved heathland in the South East. In late summer it is purple with heather. In the spring it can be dominated by yellow gorse but it varies a lot from year to year – 2022 was very disappointing, possibly due to frost damage, while 2023 was spectacular.

Ashdown forest became wooded after the last ice age and the clearance of trees to create heathland is down to man. It is unclear exactly when this occurred but certainly before medieval times when the area became a royal hunting ground. In 1372 it was given by Edward III to John of Gaunt but local residents retained their long-held rights to graze their animals and collect firewood from the forest. Charles II tried to introduce cultivation to the forest but the commoners who held the grazing rights fought back, tearing down the fences, so a Royal Commission was established that in 1693 confirmed their rights over 6400 acres of the forest.

There were further disputes resulting in an Act of Parliament in 1885 that set up a board of Conservators to administer the forest and protect the rights of all parties.

In 1987 the 10th Earl De La Warr who owned the forest wanted to sell up. There were fears that the land would fall into multiple ownership with adverse consequences. A campaign was launched to raise funds to enable the land to be purchased as a single entity for the public benefit. This was successful and the land was bought by East Sussex County Council who then placed it into a trust of which the Council is the sole trustee. However, the Council has in recent years cut back its funding of the Conservators' work, putting the proper management of the forest in jeopardy. One response to this has been the imposition of charges in almost all the forest car parks.

The forest is the setting for the adventures of Winnie-the-Pooh in the stories by A A Milne, drawing huge numbers of visitors.

Grazing is essential to maintain the heathland and the commoners don't graze sufficient animals to prevent a return to scrub and woodland. The Conservators have therefore introduced their own cattle and Exmoor ponies.

The map shows Open Access land in darker green. This corresponds broadly to the Ashdown Forest commons. The Wealdway is shown in red.

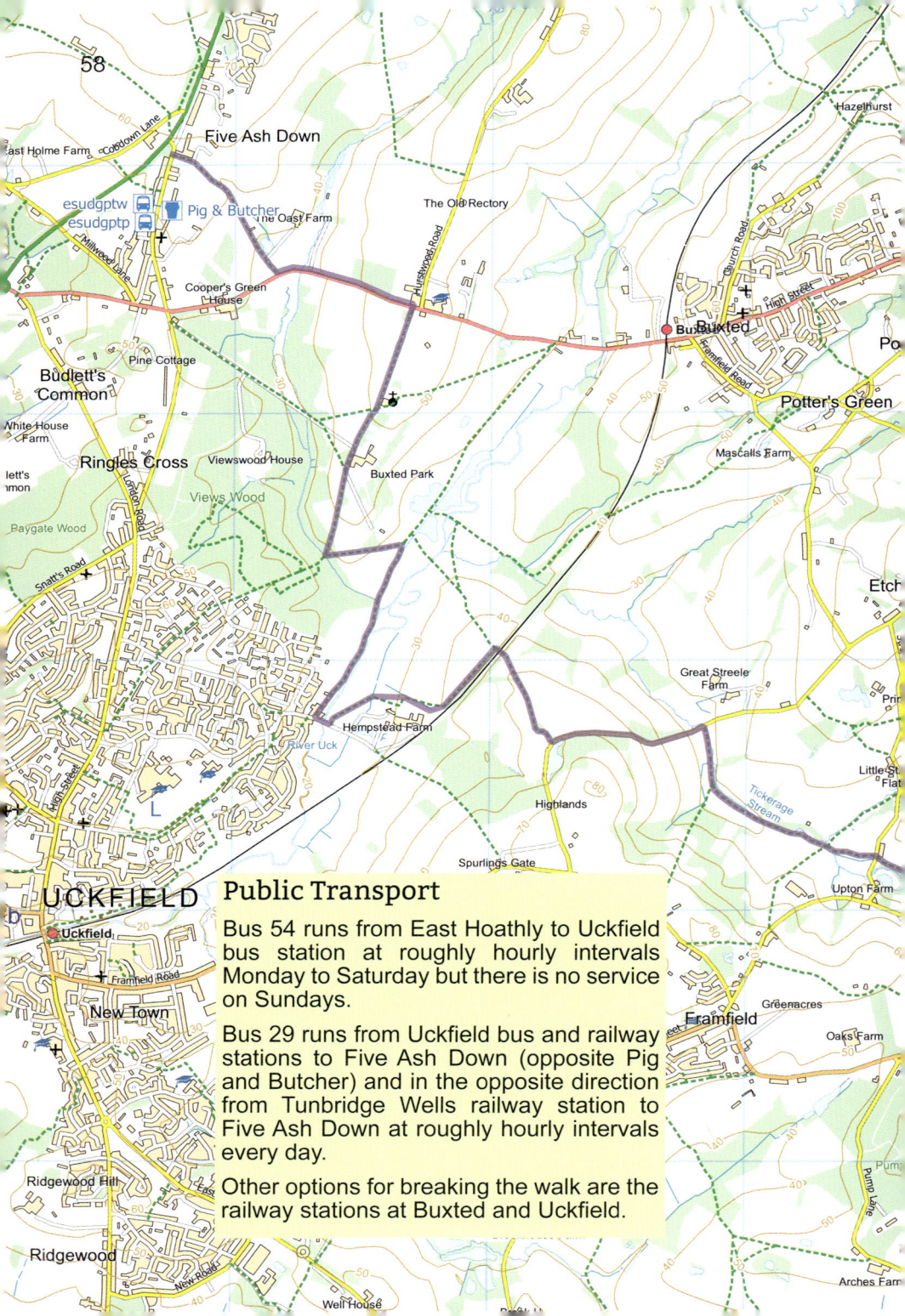

Section 7: Five Ash Down to East Hoathly (9.0 miles)

From bus stop walk up road towards A26. Just before it bends to left take signposted path on right between buildings of used vehicle centre. At far side go through pedestrian gate and along path between fence and hedge. Emerge onto small road and follow it to main road (A272).

Turn left along footway for 550 metres then cross road and follow drive for Buxted Park Hotel. Pass church of St Margaret the Queen and Buxted Park Hotel. At parking area at end of asphalt drive, go straight ahead on track initially between hedges across parkland, keep slightly right at fork away from fence and enter wood through kissing gate. On meeting track coming over raised boardwalk from right, turn left, emerge from wood and continue without change of direction to large metal gate (with sign 'Buxted Park Private Estate'). Turn right in front of it and follow path parallel to river on left, after 230 metres bearing left to footbridge. Cross bridge and keep to left along riverside path with sports pitches on right, becoming lane, to meet Hempstead Lane at T-junction.

Turn left past Hempsted Mill and cross bridge. After 70 metres take path on left between fences. After 30 metres go over stile on right (if it hasn't rotted away) and diagonally left across field to cross footbridge. Keep to right hand edge of small field then cut diagonally across the next field to gate and slightly uphill along grassy track. Cross hard area using two gates and continue forward to line of trees on railway embankment. Turn left, follow for 310 metres to meet another path coming from left and take stile on right leading to steps down to railway. Cross and take steps up other side.

Emerging into field, continue forward then soon join wide track bearing slightly right, with fence on left and, after 100 metres, hedge on right. After 175 metres as track begins to bear left, turn right through hedge and left through woodland to lane.

Turn left along lane for 600 metres and near lowest point, just before bridge with wooden railings, take path on right parallel to stream on left. Follow left hand edge of field, cross footbridge, then follow left-hand edge of two further fields to cross footbridge and gate. Turn right across narrow field, go through gate and parallel to right hand side of next field to Uptons Mill Lane.

Bear right across lane to gate and take path between hedges soon following right hand edge of two fields

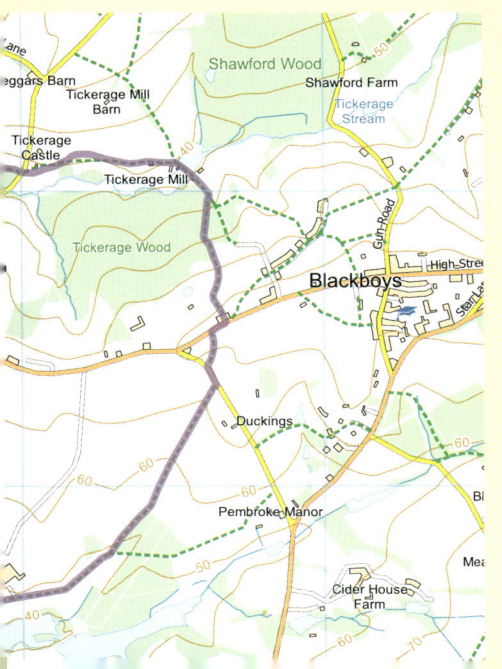

to Pound Lane.

Go over stile opposite. Soon join grassy track between paddocks and follow with hedge on left to corner of field. Bear left through gap in hedge, over footbridge and through gate into next field and follow right-hand edge to stile. Turn right along track to pass Tickeridge Mill, with mill pond on left. Some 150 metres past the mill take path on right, which swings round to left through a narrow strip of open land with electric wires above and wood on the right. On far side go over high stile and follow right hand edge of field (vineyard) to corner, cross planks into next field and follow curving left hand edge between hedge and fence to gate on left, through which follow track to road (B2102).

Cross road and turn right along footway for 55 metres. Take path on left between fence and hedge and follow to Stonebridge Lane.

Turn left for 65 metres then take path on right through gate. Bear left along left hand edge of field. When hedge ends and field opens out on left, go straight ahead to corner of wood and continue along left hand edge to corner of field. Go through gate and follow grassy track ahead, soon joining an asphalt track. Continue on the track past Newplace Farm (main house on left and various buildings on right). At corner, follow track round to left, then bear right down to Pump Lane.

Turn left and almost immediately go through gate on left. Follow left hand edge of field until woodland on left ends then maintain direction straight across middle of field to protruding corner of woodland. Continue with woodland on right to corner then go straight across field, parallel to right hand edge, to road (B2192).

Turn left along verge for 115 metres then turn right into Bushbury Lane. After just 120 metres take path on right over stile to left of two gates and head diagonally across field to stile then maintain same direction (at roughly 45 degrees to field edge) across next field to narrow strip of woodland (aim just to left of electricity pole until waymark post comes into view). Go through woodland and over footbridge. On far side, go straight along middle of field, aiming for gap in trees where power line goes through, and join Beechy Road.

Cross road and two stiles and head down field on faint path parallel to right hand hedge to kissing gate. Enter thin strip of woodland, go down to footbridge and cross stream. Head out into open field and straight up towards waymark post by solitary oak tree and turn sharp right to field boundary and footbridge. Across bridge bear slightly left, aiming for a stile in distance to right of solitary tree on field border. Pass under power lines, cross the stile and follow path into wood. Through wood head down grassy track between fence, with fine views of South Downs ahead. Join tarmac road and continue past a stud farm. Take path to left of gates then bear left down drive for 300 metres to lane.

Go straight across lane and along track to left of community garden. On reaching wood turn left along right hand edge of field and at corner continue right along stony track towards church. Pass to right of church then keep left through churchyard to Church Marks Lane and on to High Street at East Hoathly. Turn left for bus stop and continue past bus stop for next section of walk.

Points of Interest

Hogge House

As you turn off the main road into Buxted Park, Hogge House is on the corner on the left hand side of the drive. If you venture briefly along the main road, turn left up Hurstwood Road for a few metres and then look back at the house you will see on the wall above the door a cast iron image of a pig over the date 1581. The is the "rebus" of Ralph Hogge, a prominent Tudor ironmaster who died in 1585. He is said to have been the first to cast a cannon in England, apparently while working for William Levett, the Rector of Buxted, who owned several iron foundries in the Weald in England. He later became the Queen's "gonnestonemaker" – her manufacturer of cannon balls.

Buxted Park

The village of Buxted was once located close to the mansion and the old church but in the 1830s the owner, Lord Liverpool, wanted more privacy and decided to move the village outside the park.

Buxted Park

The villagers refused to go so Lord Liverpool stopped maintaining the village houses until they became uninhabitable and the villagers had no option but to comply. The village is still at its new location close to the railway, probably too far from the Wealdway for a quick detour to the pub but close enough for access to public transport if you wish to break your expedition here.

The mansion was completed in 1725, bought in 1931 by architect Basil Ionides and gutted by fire in 1940. Ionides substantially reconstructed the house using fittings salvaged from other houses being demolished or damaged during the blitz. The house is now a hotel and conference centre.

Church of St Margaret the Queen

The size of the church, built about 1250, reflects the village that once existed nearby and the wider area it served. St Margaret was queen of Scotland in the eleventh century and three of her sons became Kings of Scotland.

Uckfield

As the Wealdway passes within a mile of Uckfield railway station, the town offers another option for accessing public transport. There are also buses to East Hoathly, Upper Horsebridge and Hailsham.

The town has held a market since 1280 and was a centre of the Wealden iron industry and later the Sussex tile, brick and pottery industry. There are no exceptional buildings but the town can apparently claim fame for the last verified sighting of Lord Lucan before his complete disappearance.

Blackboys

The village grew around the Blackboys Inn, a 14th century coaching inn. There are many theories as to the origin of the name including the appearance of local charcoal burners after a day's work, a variation on Black Wood or Blake's Wood or a variation on the name of 14th century resident Richard Blakeboy.

Framfield

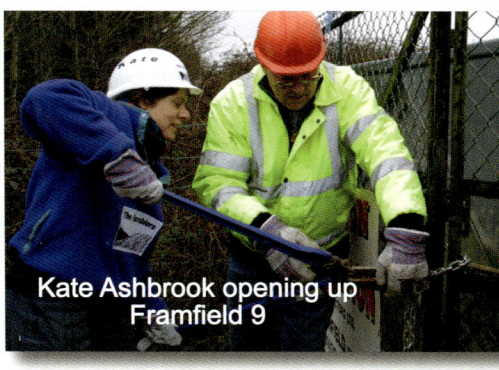

Kate Ashbrook opening up Framfield 9

The name of this quiet parish has gone down in the annals of walking history because here a famous victory was won in 2003. Notorious property tycoon Nicholas van Hoogstraten, through a company called Rarebargain, bought an estate here and began building a mansion known as Hamilton Palace. He also obstructed a footpath known as Framfield 9 in order to keep walkers off his land. The County Council failed to remove the obstruction, preferring a diversion, and it was left to the Ramblers and Open Spaces Society General Secretary Kate Ashbrook to take legal action to have the path opened up. Despite £40m having allegedly been spent on the mansion, van Hoogstraten fled the country leaving the half-built property to the mercy of the elements and it remains abandoned and decaying to this day.

Tickerage Mill

Originally the site of a furnace and forge and later a corn mill, in more recent times the house has been home to several famous people, most notably actress Vivien Leigh of Gone with the Wind fame after her divorce from Lawrence Olivier in 1960. Other former occupants include artist Richard Wyndham who wrote the 1940 Batsford guide to South East England and Sir Ronald Armstrong Jones, father of Lord Snowdon.

Newplace Farm

The large ponds are relics of the Wealden iron industry which held water to drive the bellows pumping air into the furnace. There are mine pits from which iron ore was dug in the Wadhurst clay in the nearby woods.

Old Whyly

Until the 20th century known simply as Whyly or Wilegh, the house was long the home of the Lunsford family. The most infamous member of the family was Sir Thomas. In 1632 he tried to kill his cousin and neighbour Sir Thomas Pelham, on whose estate he had been caught poaching and fined, by shooting him as he emerged from the door of East Hoathly church – but missed. He was imprisoned for the crime in Newgate but escaped and fled to France. He returned, was pardoned by Charles I, fought on the Royalist side in the Civil War and finally emigrated to Virginia.

Section 8: East Hoathly to Upper Horsebridge (6.1 miles)

From bus stop head north-east along High Street away from church, for 180 metres then right along Buttsfield Lane. Keep left at "The Old Post Office" (marked number 10 on gate post) and follow narrow lane eventually becoming unsurfaced, crossing private drive and continuing on path between fences. On entering wood, bear left and then right and after emerging from wood follow left hand edge of two fields to Graywood Lane.

Take path almost opposite across middle of field and maintain direction in next field. When field narrows, follow right hand edge. Maintain direction to gate into next field and soon join stony track passing house on right then bearing right past Frith's Farm and after 300 metres reaching Highland's Lane. Turn left and follow lane for 550 metres to centre of Chiddingly. As lane bends right at Six Bells pub, maintain forward direction along narrower lane and follow round to right. On reaching church, bear left and soon take path through pedestrian gate into field. Bear right diagonally across two fields to far corner. Go over stile, follow path down to stream and across bridge, go through narrow strip of woodland,

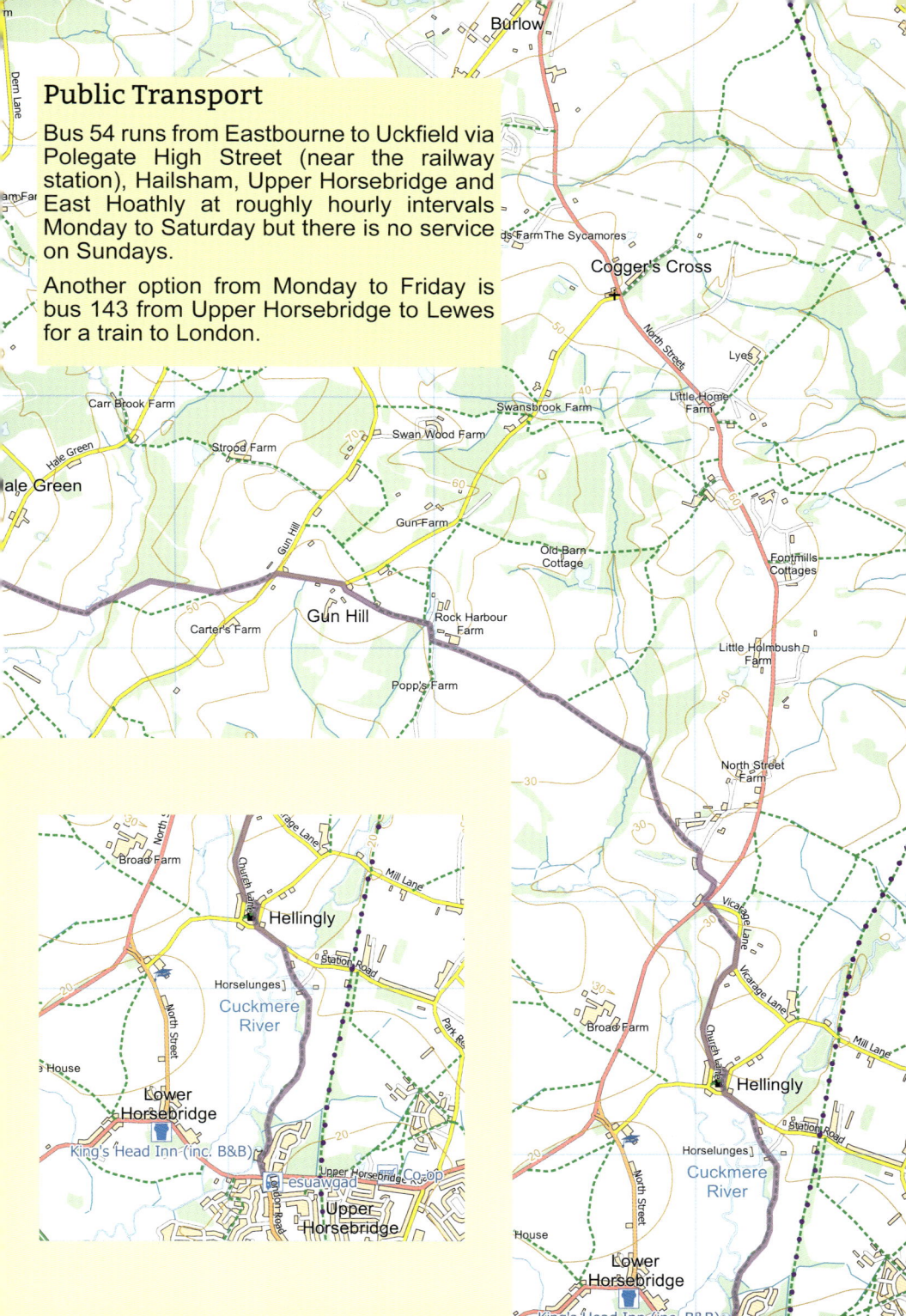

over stile, straight across field and through kissing gate in corner.

Turn left along Scraper's Hill for 35 metres and take track on right along left hand edges of two fields to footbridge over stream. Cross and take path across field and then through narrow strip of woodland. Follow path along grassy left hand margin of field to far left corner (this is likely to be easier than the strict line of the path across the middle of the field). Continue across next field, emerging onto Gun Hill over stile.

Turn left for just a few metres then right along Swansbrook Lane. When lane bears left maintain forward direction along stony track for 350 metres to T-junction by pond at West Street Farm. Turn right and take first left just after Rock Harbour Farm, initially along left hand edge of field then bearing slightly right to stile 25m from top corner of field. Cross next field to stile then follow left hand edge of field to copse. Go through, turn right keeping copse on your right then continue in same direction to cross narrow field and follow right hand edge of next field to wood. Follow path into ghyll, cross footbridge and bear right as you climb out of wood. Continue across meadow, over bridge, between fence and hedge, cross a small field and a private drive and go down some steps to North Lane. Turn right and follow round left hand bend to road (A267) on edge of Hellingly.

Follow narrow tarred track on right to houses then cross A267 onto Vicarage Lane opposite and almost immediately take path through gate on right. Bear left across field, soon rejoining Vicarage Lane over a stile by a field gate. Turn right and at first junction keep right along Church Lane. Carry on until you reach Hellingly church and enter churchyard as road bends right. Follow path clockwise round churchyard to opposite corner and emerge on Mill Lane. Turn right and immediately left along Station Road.

Immediately after crossing metal-railed bridge, take path on right and cross field diagonally to gate. Follow path through scrub, cross moat around Horselunges Manor and emerge onto forecourt with pond on left. Cross forecourt and take path to left of garages. Bear left into field then right along right hand edge of field to corner. Go through gap in hedge on right to edge of Cuckmere River, turn left through gate and continue straight ahead through trees, passing old flour mill and joining rough lane to Upper Horsebridge Road.

Hellingly

Points of Interest

East Hoathly

Thanks to a 1992 bypass of the A22, the compact village has shed its claim to stand on the worst main-road bend in Sussex and is now pleasant and peaceful with a pub and a few shops. The church boasts a 15th century "Pelham Tower" built by the local Pelham family – the others are in nearby Laughton and Chiddingly but the designs are far from identical. The rest of the church was rebuilt in 1855. The correct pronunciation of the three villages passed on this section of the walk is suggested by the old saying "Hellingly, Chiddingly and East Hoathly – three lies and all true".

Jefferay House

This building, part of a once larger mansion, which you pass as you approach Chiddingly, was built by Sir John Jefferay, Elizabeth I's Lord Chief Baron of the Exchequer who died in 1578. He was a lawyer who acted for the Crown in a dispute over grazing rights on nearby Dicker common which was owned by the Duchy of Lancaster. He appeared, however, to favour the interests of the Crown's opponents including members of the Pelham family (see above) with whom he was thought to be in collusion. He was MP for various constituencies including Clitheroe in Lancashire and East Grinstead. There is a splendid marble memorial to Jefferay in Chiddingly church. The house has previously been known as Chiddingly Place and Place Farmhouse.

Chiddingly

Now one of the quietest spots for miles around, in the 17th century it was a busy centre of the Wealden iron industry with Stream furnace nearby where the Fuller family cast cannon, bells and firebacks. A cannon-boring bar was found here which was used to inform the reconstruction of a boring mill for the Anne of Cleves House museum in Lewes. The church, of varying dates, is unusual for the area in having a stone rather than wooden shingle spire atop its 15th century tower.

Hellingly

Hellingly is a gem of a village. The church is built atop a circular Saxon burial mound and the houses are built around it, those on the north side fronting directly onto the churchyard to form a charmingly picturesque group. Parts of the church date from about 1190, most is 15th century and the bell tower was added in 1836 to replace "a mean wooden spire".

Horselunges Manor

Opinions vary as to the origin of the name – perhaps a combination of two names, de Herst and Lyngyver, two 14th century owners of an earlier house. The 15th century timber-framed house, built by the Devenish family, is surrounded by a moat which some say is fed by a spring and others by the Cuckmere River.

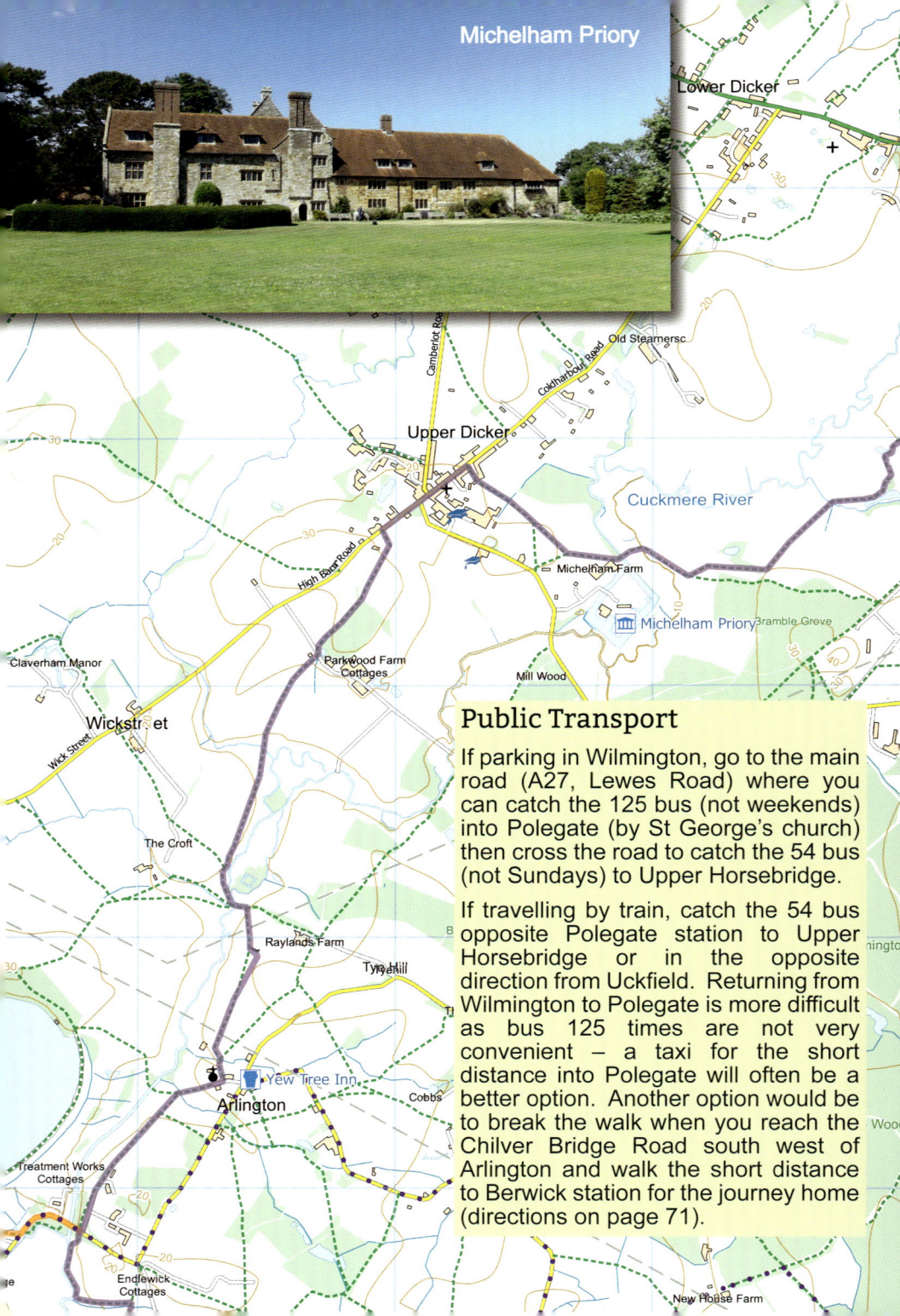

Public Transport

If parking in Wilmington, go to the main road (A27, Lewes Road) where you can catch the 125 bus (not weekends) into Polegate (by St George's church) then cross the road to catch the 54 bus (not Sundays) to Upper Horsebridge.

If travelling by train, catch the 54 bus opposite Polegate station to Upper Horsebridge or in the opposite direction from Uckfield. Returning from Wilmington to Polegate is more difficult as bus 125 times are not very convenient – a taxi for the short distance into Polegate will often be a better option. Another option would be to break the walk when you reach the Chilver Bridge Road south west of Arlington and walk the short distance to Berwick station for the journey home (directions on page 71).

Bede's School, Upper Dicker

Section 9: Upper Horsebridge to Wilmington (7.1 miles)

Head west along south side of Upper Horsebridge Road for 120 metres from junction with London Road then turn left into Cuckmere Close. After 85 metres turn left across verge into Sheppey Walk. After 50 metres take path on right between fences and follow, crossing Shetland Close and Lundy Walk, emerging into open grassy area. Follow hard path across footbridge and turn left with ditch on left. After 50 metres take first right turn soon gently uphill following Aspinall Grove with houses on right and field then community centre on left. At top turn right along Brunel Drive and at corner take path sharp left along hard track with houses on left and hedge on right. Reaching green play area on left, take path up bank on right and go over stile in hedge to bypass. Cross dual carriageway (A22) to Wealdway finger post and turn left along verge. At next Wealdway fingerpost take path over stile right.

Follow left hand edge of field to corner and go over footbridge and stile on left. Bear left over another stile and follow direction of arrow on post, aiming slightly to left of clump of large bushes (the field is rather overgrown at time of writing). Soon continue forward between bushes and hedge, then cross stile. On emerging into open field, turn right and follow right hand edge, gradually curving left past pond on right, to corner. Enter another field and follow right hand edge to second pond (with lilies and private fishing sign). Go through gap into next field and bear left along two sides of field to second corner. Go over stile into next field and head half right for stile visible across marshy field (half way along curving course of stream) and a footbridge.

Head straight across field to middle of far side following faint path looking for WW fingerpost which becomes visible halfway across (in line with protruding corner of wood). Go over

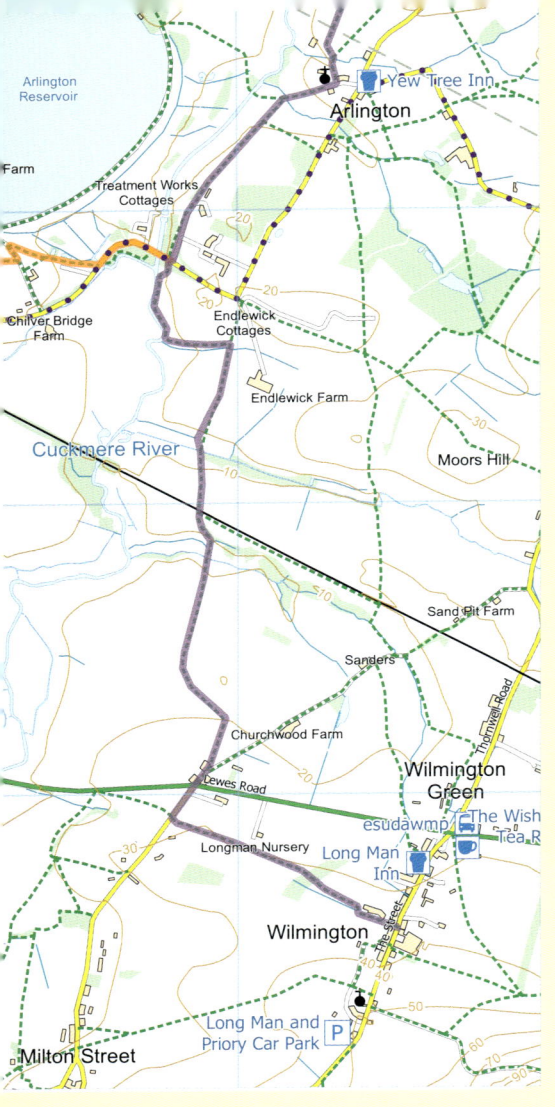

field to top corner. Go over stile and bear right along right hand edge of school playing fields. When hedge starts to bear right at clump of bushes, go straight ahead across playing field to bridge near middle of far side. Continue in same direction on rough ground then passing between houses and emerging on Coldharbour Road at Upper Dicker.

Turn left along road for 425 metres passing Bede's School and The Plough public house. Shortly after pub, take path on left between hedges. Soon enter field and turn right along right hand edges of plantation and playing field to stile. Go over and along left hand edge of next field to asphalt track.

Turn left for a few metres then take path on right over stile by gate. Cross field to stile in hedge on far side (where chalk track goes through hedge) and continue in same direction crossing next field to stile in hedge somewhat to left of far right corner. Continue straight across next field to footbridge. Over bridge the route strictly goes straight ahead across very large field to far left corner (if field cropped it may be easier to turn left and follow field edge to far corner). At corner go over stile and bear left towards narrowing point of field to track and bridges over Cuckmere River. Cross stile and footbridge, then turn left and cross larger bridge over Cuckmere. After 50 metres turn sharp right over a stile, cross field under power lines, aiming just to right of building at top. Go through gate, keep forward along short edge of field for 40 metres to corner and turn right along long edge of field to cross stile in corner. Over stile, take path on left across corner of next field then into churchyard, emerging at far left corner on The

stile. Continue through narrow strip of wood, bear diagonally across narrow field to far corner and go over stile on left into field then follow right hand edge to stile and go over. Walk full length of narrow field to join track and turn left toward bridge over River Cuckmere. Michelham Priory is across the moat on your left but not visible.

Immediately before first farm building on right, bear right diagonally across

Street at Arlington.

Turn right along gravel track then go over stile into field. Cross diagonally to footbridge and on far side cross middle of field parallel to right hand edge, following sign to Wilmington Church. Continue across next field parallel to River Cuckmere below on the right. Aim just to the right of the buildings ahead and after passing between rows of trees join asphalt track in front of house and bear right along track to lane (Chilver Bridge Road).

Turn right for a few metres and just before bridge take path on left, cross stile and follow along right hand edge of field with river just below on right. On reaching hedge at field corner turn left to top of field. Go though hedge at corner, turn right along track and through gate to follow right hand edge of field. Nearing end of field, bear left to join track not far away and follow to railway. Cross carefully and follow track bearing left then right down to footbridge. Cross stream over broken stile, follow grassy track a few metres uphill and keep left on field edge to corner. Go left through gap into next field and now follow right hand hedge to gap between hedges. Turn right and continue along rough track through gates and past buildings to meet A27 Lewes Road.

Cross road with care and go straight ahead up lane (Milton Street). In 200 metres take path on left just before first house. Follow path first between hedges, then across a field and in same direction across another field into wood. On far side follow path between hedge and fence. Emerge briefly along left hand edge of field and continue to corner. Ignore waymark on post pointing right along field edge and take less obvious path forward through woodland and over footbridge soon emerging on The Street at Wilmington. Turn left for bus stops or right to continue along the Wealdway.

Link Route to Berwick Station (0.9 miles)

Turn right down Chilver Bridge Road crossing bridge over River Cuckmere. Soon after road bends left, and opposite layby on left, turn right over stile following footpath sign.

Cross small field heading for stile in left hand corner. Continue on path in woodland soon reaching another stile. Cross and continue in same direction slightly uphill to footpath sign, bear left and cross stile onto track. Turn left for 70 metres then turn right through initially hidden gate into field. Follow left hand edge of field uphill and through gate. Continue along left hand fence turning left downhill to reach hedge.

Cross small bridge with gate each side and continue on path under pylons to another gate. Continue in same direction, go through gate and between houses to reach Station Road. The station is across road to left.

Approaching the South Downs

Points of Interest

Michelham Priory

Here are the remains of an Augustinian Priory founded in 1229, possibly on the site of a former moated Norman manor house. The priory was dissolved by Henry VIII in 1536 and much of the complex of buildings, including the church, has been demolished with the original layout marked out in the garden. The main surviving building has a Tudor exterior but older work survives inside. The large barn housing a forge has a 19th century exterior but may be 17th century internally. There is a gatehouse consisting of a 15th century tower and a 16th century bridge across the moat.

The moat, reputedly England's largest, is fed by water from the river Cuckmere. This has become unreliable lately so that at times there is little or no water in parts of the moat.

The site belongs to Sussex Archaeological Society and is worth a visit. It is closed in January and February and opens weekends only in December. There is a tea room.

Upper Dicker

The village is dominated by Bede's Senior School, many of whose buildings are part of "The Dicker" estate assembled by Horatio Bottomley MP who was notorious for his dubious business enterprises and downright frauds in the late 19th and early 20th centuries. The Wealdway passes Bottomley's former front door, now bearing a brass plate as the registered office of St Bede's School Trust (the school dropped the "St" from its name in 2012).

Holy Trinity church, built in 1843, is reputed to have a fine west window.

Arlington

The church has a long history with features of all architectural periods from Saxon onwards. During restoration around 1890 traces of burnt clay from a wattle and daub wall were found suggesting the remains of an earlier building, perhaps even Roman.

The church appears a rather splendid affair for the tiny village we see today but in medieval times the village was far larger and as you continue your journey south west away from the church you are passing the buried foundations of the abandoned part of the village.

Arlington church viewed across the site of the abandoned medieval village

Arlington Reservoir

After leaving Arlington church you will see in the distance on your right the embankment holding back the contents of the reservoir which was built in 1971. As the water level is above the immediately surrounding countryside, you will not be able to see the water surface until you climb the South Downs by the Wilmington Long Man.

Wilmington

Cuckmere River

The Cuckmere is one of several rivers draining waters from the Weald and cutting through the South Downs to the English Channel. The water meadows created as they meander through the chalk were an important component of the traditional sheep and corn farming that sustained the local population for hundreds, perhaps thousands, of years. Without dung from the sheep the thin soils of the chalk were quickly leached of nutrients and so the sheep would be brought every night onto the arable fields to tread in their dung and were returned to pasture every morning. Downland pasture would be poor in early spring and the water meadows filled the gap, allowing more sheep to be overwintered than would otherwise have been the case.

The Cuckmere is the only major river in Sussex that remains undeveloped at its mouth. Between 1740 and 1840 Cuckmere Haven was a magnet for smugglers and it is said that in the 1780s up to 300 men might be there at one time taking goods from the beach with a dozen smuggling vessels waiting offshore.

Link Route from Berwick Station (0.9 miles)

From platform 2 cross station concourse to Station Road. Cross over and almost immediately turn right following footpath sign to left of Berwick Service Station passing between houses. Go through gate and bear slightly left following path towards telegraph pole. Go through another gate and continue underneath telegraph wires to gate, footbridge and gate in hedge.

Follow path uphill with fence on your right. At top of hill bear right with fence to another gate. There are fine views of Arlington Reservoir to the left and the Downs to the right. Go through gate and down next field, again to right of field edge.

Pass through gate in the corner of the field and turn left up a track. In 70 metres, where the hedge on right ends and just before a wide gate, turn right over a stile.

Continue forward for 30 metres then bear right following footpath sign down field to stile in hedge. After short stretch on path through woodland cross another stile and continue in same direction across small field, aiming for stile to right of leaning tree in hedge.

Cross stile onto Chilver Bridge Road and turn left. Just after crossing bridge over the Cuckmere turn right to continue along Wealdway.

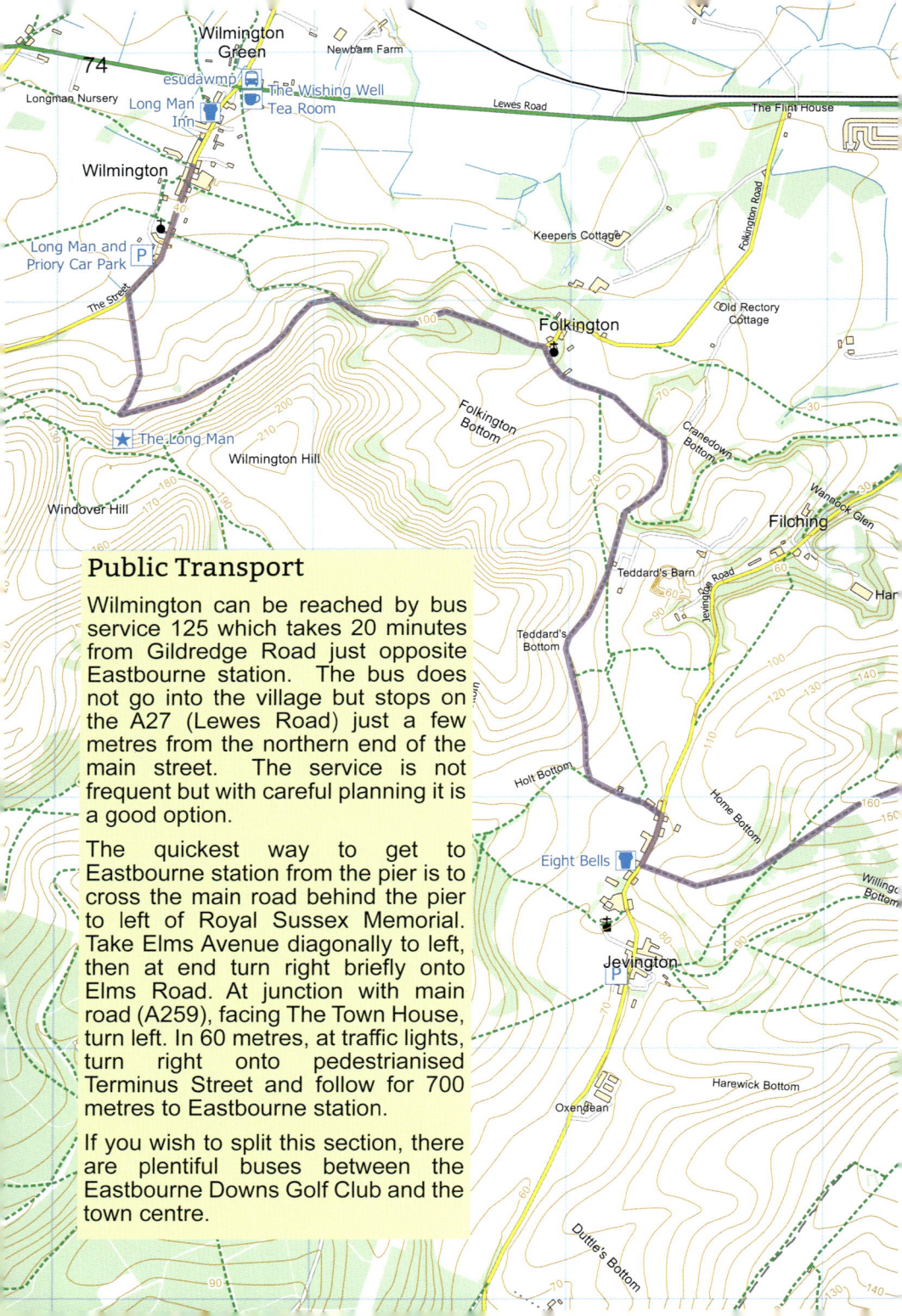

Public Transport

Wilmington can be reached by bus service 125 which takes 20 minutes from Gildredge Road just opposite Eastbourne station. The bus does not go into the village but stops on the A27 (Lewes Road) just a few metres from the northern end of the main street. The service is not frequent but with careful planning it is a good option.

The quickest way to get to Eastbourne station from the pier is to cross the main road behind the pier to left of Royal Sussex Memorial. Take Elms Avenue diagonally to left, then at end turn right briefly onto Elms Road. At junction with main road (A259), facing The Town House, turn left. In 60 metres, at traffic lights, turn right onto pedestrianised Terminus Street and follow for 700 metres to Eastbourne station.

If you wish to split this section, there are plentiful buses between the Eastbourne Downs Golf Club and the town centre.

Section 10: Wilmington to Eastbourne (10.3 miles)

Head south along The Street for 500 metres past church and priory. Immediately opposite car park on right, take path on left running parallel to road. At barrier turn left along bridleway climbing towards human figure marked on hillside. Go through gate and continue in same direction. Immediately beneath figure by information board turn left along side of downs. Pass bottom of wooded area and on reaching broader track (byway) at T-junction, turn right through wood and follow all the way to junction of paths at edge of Folkington.

Church and village are very close along lane on left but our route goes down rough chalky track ahead. Follow track, often between hedges, for 1.3 miles to T-junction. Turn left and soon arrive at Jevington Road.

Turn right for 220 metres to Eight Bells pub then take path on left up steps behind bus stop. Follow path between fences climbing steeply then alongside fence to join track climbing to left up open downland. At waymark post take right fork towards stile visible ahead. Cross stile and follow path along right flank of ridge with wide views of downs on right. Cross another stile and pass between bushes, later with fence on right. When path bears slightly right continue ahead to escarpment with view across Willingdon, Eastbourne and the sea. Turn right, rejoin earlier path and follow edge of fence along southbound ridge keeping to right of knoll. Go through a gate to left of a field gate and continue with fence now on left. Go through another gate next to a field gate, passing bottom of Butts Lane car park, and in a few metres fork right onto chalky track until you reach South Downs Way at a prominent fingerpost. (From this point the Wealdway and the South Downs Way coincide so you can follow signage for either route.) Turn left to follow SDW along easternmost ridge southwards with views across Eastbourne on left. Follow track through golf course.

On reaching A259 (where you can take refreshment at golf club house), bear right to crossing point and continue on far side. Stay on main path signed SDW. After 350 metres fork right and soon reach trig point and small concrete pond with benches. Bear right and soon at cross paths bear left along edge of wood, following SDW sign, and descend gradually to Warren Hill, B2103, at junction with minor road. Bear left to crossing point, cross and bear left uphill to ridge following the SDW. On reaching triangular junction of paths where there is no forward option you could bear right to visit Beachy Head then make your own way to Eastbourne by one of many available paths. If sticking to the Wealdway, bear left downhill. Just before path comes in from left, take right hand fork and keep descending to The Kiosk (refreshments).

Go straight ahead down Dukes Road past Helen Garden on right (where toilet and refreshment facilities stay open later than The Kiosk) then take first right, Holywell Drive, down to promenade (where more toilet and refreshment opportunities are available). Turn left and follow to pier.

Congratulations on reaching the end of your adventure.

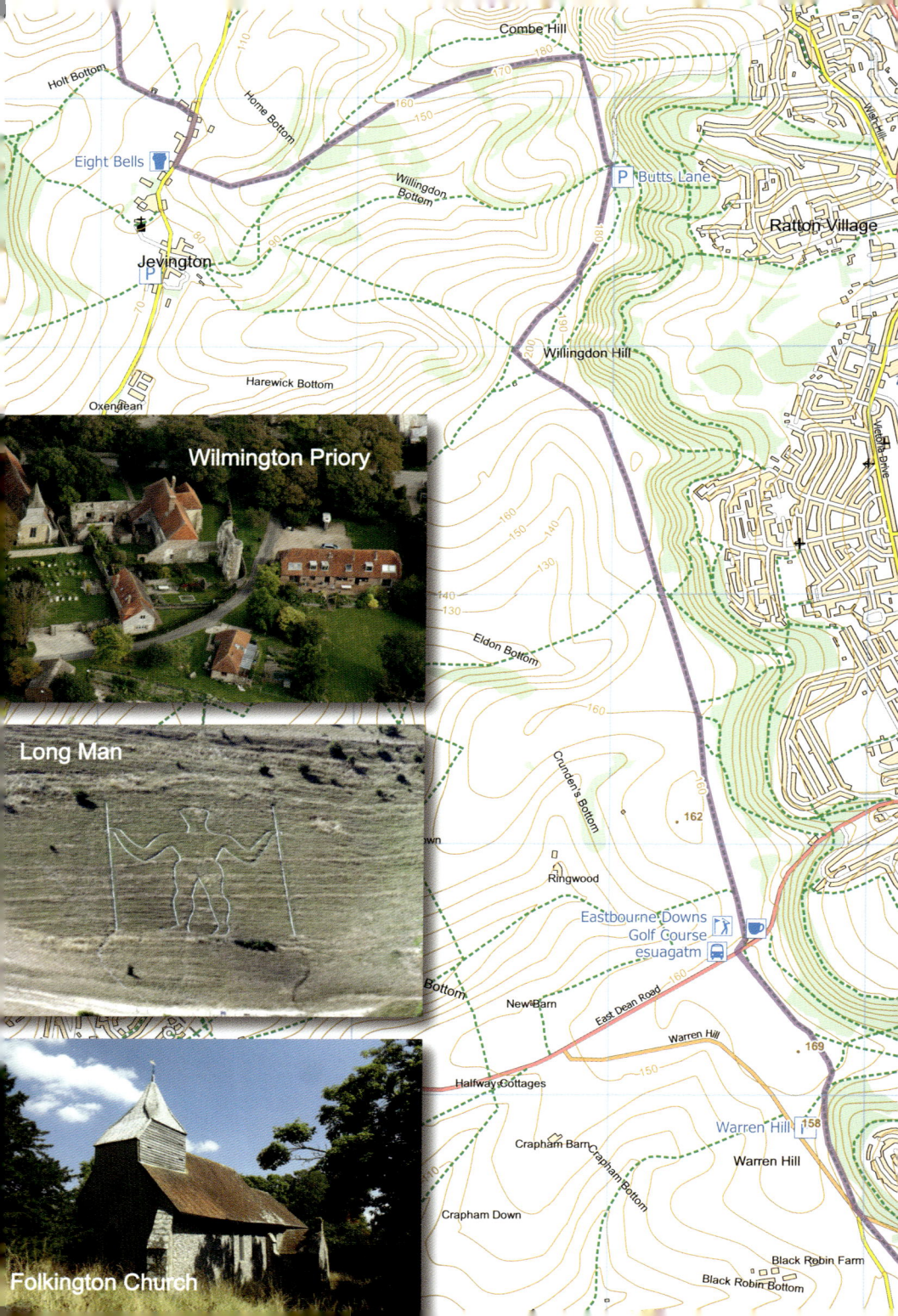

Points of Interest

Wilmington

A most attractive village consisting of a single street. The pub, previously called the Giant's Rest, has recently been refurbished and has reopened as the Long Man Inn.

Wilmington Priory

The priory was founded soon after the Norman conquest by King William's half brother, Robert de Mortain, and was the property of the Norman abbey of Grestain until given in 1483 to Chichester Cathedral who in 1565 granted it to Sir Richard Sackville. The estate then passed through various hands until it reached the ninth Duke of Devonshire who in 1925 gave it to the Sussex Archaeological Society. It was open to the public every summer with an agricultural museum upstairs until at least 1980 but is now owned by the Landmark Trust who let it out as holiday accommodation. It is open to the public on just two days a year.

Wilmington Church

The flint-walled church adjoins the remains of the Priory and was shared between the monks and the parishioners. The nave is Norman with a king post roof. The wooden pulpit is Jacobean. The original stained glass window in the north chapel (13th century?) depicting St Peter surrounded by British butterflies and bees was destroyed by fire in 2002 and has been replaced by a modern window with a similar theme. Outside a yew, said to be much older than the church, is supported on a large number of wooden props. The church is of sufficient interest to be Grade I listed.

The Long Man

Once thought prehistoric, the figure is now considered to be a 16th or 17th century creation. Originally scarcely visible as a depression in the grass and known as "the green man", the figure was reconfigured with whitewashed yellow bricks in 1873-4 and these were replaced with breeze blocks in 1969. The soil is too deep to allow the outline to be cut right down to the chalk.

In 2021 during the Covid-19 outbreak a face mask was painted onto the figure; it is not there now.

Folkington

This small hamlet is pronounced "Fowington". Just a minute's detour from the Wealdway is the tiny 13th century church dedicated to St Peter Ad Vincula which means "St Peter in chains" and alludes to a biblical story about the liberation of Peter the Apostle by an angel when held prisoner by King Herod Agrippa. The overgrown graveyard contains the grave of Elizabeth David, the celebrated cookery writer, who grew up in the village. The flint and rubble church contains enough points of interest to be Grade I listed.

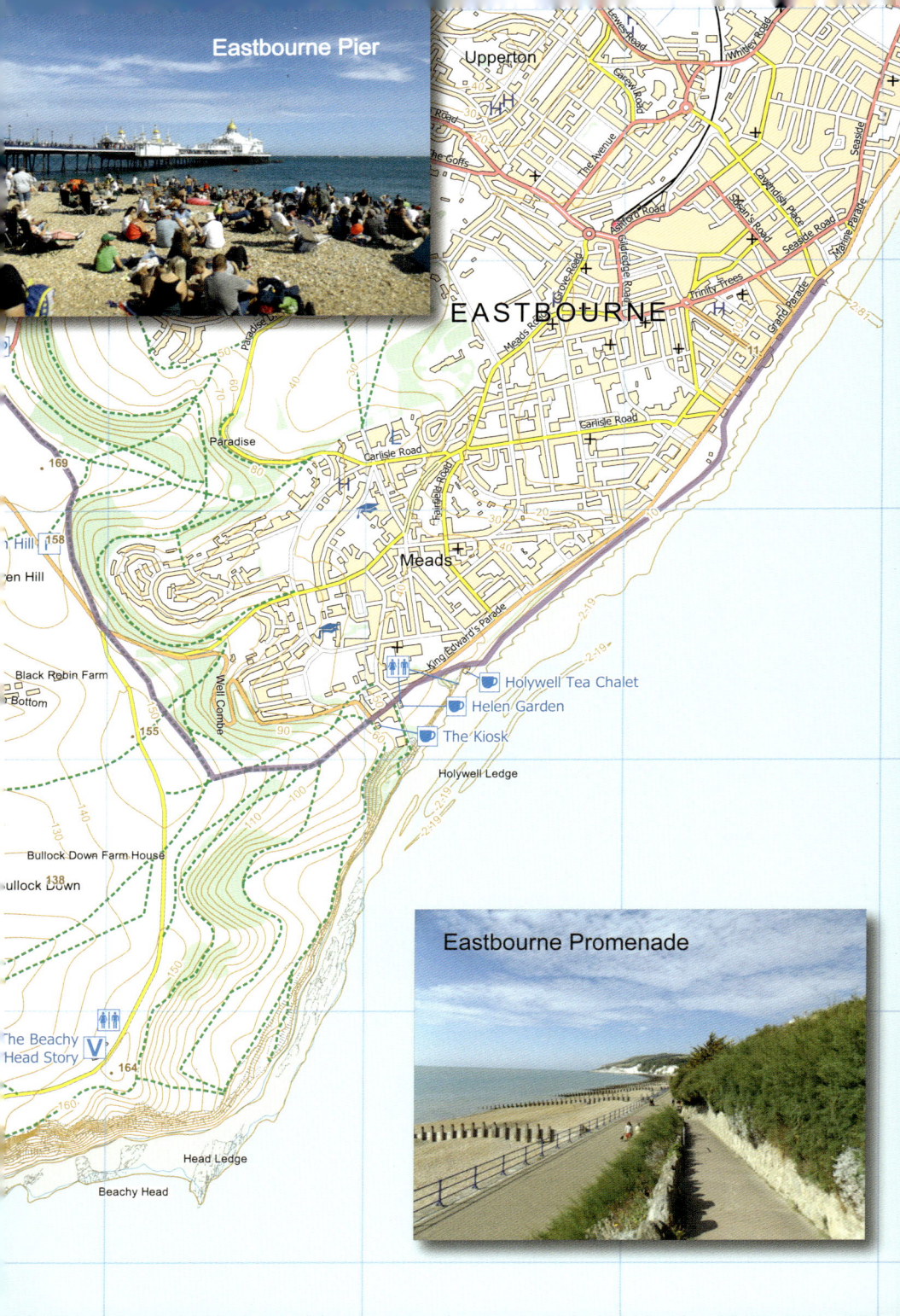

Jevington

The route of the Wealdway gives only a glimpse of the village so for a full appreciation of its character you will need to venture along the road past the Eight Bells pub and then return to continue on your way. Human settlement here goes back a long way. In the hills around the village are many barrows and there was a neolithic settlement nearby. A Roman road came over the downs from Willingdon, apparently ending in the village just where the Wealdway joined the main street. A monastery was founded here in 1344 and dissolved in 1538 by Henry VIII. The village was a hot spot for smuggling, the local gang being led by a villager known as "Jevington Jigg" who was convicted of horse stealing in 1799 and deported to Botany Bay, never to return. While in Jevington he lived in a house that later became the Hungry Monk restaurant where Banoffee Pie was invented in 1974; it is now closed.

The church has a Saxon tower and is an atmospheric landmark visible from a wide swathe of surrounding downland.

Beachy Head

The Wealdway route described here does not pass Beachy Head. The famous landmark can nevertheless by visited by a short diversion from the route just before the final descent into Eastbourne. There is a visitor centre with interesting information about the landscape, its history and its ecology. The clifftop is likely to be teeming with visitors who arrive by the busload but most of whom don't stray very far from the main viewpoint. The name of the 534 ft high cliff comes from the Norman French "Beau Chef" meaning beautiful headland.

Eastbourne

The town is said to enjoy more sunshine than any other English coastal resort. It became popular largely after 1850 when landowner, the seventh Duke of Devonshire, decided to develop the seafront area which is landscaped with a three-tiered promenade.

The pier is a grand Victorian affair with glass and golden domes. It was built in 1888 and extends 1000 feet out to sea. The third of the pier nearest land was badly damaged by fire in 2014 but has been fully repaired.

Eastbourne Air Show

One of the main events in Eastbourne's calendar is the International Air Show, held every year in August. The show can conveniently be seen from the hills around the town, especially from the Wealdway just before descending from the Downs.

Acknowledgements

Thanks are due to the many people have helped with this book by testing the route directions or checking the text.

Mapping

Contains OS data © Crown copyright and database rights (2023).

Contains British Geological Survey materials © UKRI 2020

The base mapping is derived from Ordnance Survey data released into the public domain under the Open Government Licence. Geological maps and features are derived from BGS data released under the Open Government licence.

The footpaths in Kent and East Sussex are derived from data released by the respective county councils under the Open Government licence.

The national and regional cycle networks are reproduced by kind permission of Sustrans.

The routes of the walks are based on GPS tracks made by the author.

All other information on the maps has been created by the author.

Photographs and Illustrations

Page 23: Photograph of Luddesdown courtesy of Jack Yan

Page 24: Lower photograph courtesy of Cee and Dave Wetton

Page 76: Wilmington Priory. Barbara van Cleve. Creative Commons Attribution-ShareAlike 3.0 Unported (CC BY-SA 3.0)

About the Ramblers

The Ramblers exists to encourage walking and support walkers. It does this by organising led walks, by publicising and promoting walking opportunities and most importantly by protecting our rights of access on foot in both town and countryside. The vast majority of what we do is done by volunteers who lead walks, write guidebooks, maintain websites, clear blocked paths and spend hours poring over legal documents and maps to ensure that unsatisfactory proposals for diverting and closing paths are effectively challenged and to identify rights of way omitted from local authority "definitive" maps.

Footpath between Folkestone and Dover saved from closure by the Ramblers

Whether you like led walks or prefer to go it alone, please support us by being a member – or better still by also becoming one of our volunteers.